HELEN HOPE MIRRLEES was bo...
Kent. She grew up in Scotland and was educated ...
School in St Andrews. She briefly attended the Royal Academy of
Dramatic Art before entering Newnham College, Cambridge in
1910, to study classics. There she met the classics scholar Jane Ellen
Harrison (1850-1928) and the two women became companions
until Harrison's death. Hope visited Paris intermittently from 1913
onwards, before taking up residence there with Harrison in 1922.
The two women studied Russian at the École des Langues
Orientales and translated two works from the Russian: *The Life of
the Archpriest Avvakum by Himself* (1924) and *The Book of the Bear*, a
collection of Russian folktales (1926). Hope's first novel, *Madeleine:
One of Love's Jansenists* (1919) was followed by her long poem *Paris*,
published by the Hogarth Press in 1920. Two other novels were
published in the 1920s, *The Counterplot* (1924) and the fantasy novel
Lud-in-the-Mist (1926). After Jane Harrison's death, Hope
converted to Catholicism and, in the 1940s, moved to South Africa.
She did not publish again until 1962, with *A Fly in Amber*, a biog-
raphy of the British antiquarian Sir Robert Bruce Cotton. Three slim
volumes of her poetry appeared during these later years, which
culminated in the Amate Press edition of *Moods and Tensions* (1976),
introduced by Raymond Mortimer. In later life, she returned to
England and died at the age of ninety-one on 1 August 1978.

SANDEEP PARMAR received her PhD in English Literature from
University College London in 2008. She has written extensively on
the unpublished autobiographies of the modernist poet Mina Loy.
She is currently writing Hope Mirrlees's biography and editing her
out-of-print novels at Clare Hall, Cambridge, where she is a
Visiting Fellow. From 2009 to 2010 she was a Visiting Scholar at the
Center for the Study of Gender and Sexuality at New York
University.

JULIA BRIGGS OBE was Professor of Literature and Women's Studies
at De Montfort University. Among her many influential publica-
tions were a biography of E. Nesbit and her acclaimed *Virginia
Woolf: An Inner Life*. She died in 2007.

Fyfield*Books* aim to make available some of the great classics of British and European literature in clear, affordable formats, and to restore often neglected writers to their place in literary tradition.

Fyfield*Books* take their name from the Fyfield elm in Matthew Arnold's 'Scholar Gypsy' and 'Thyrsis'. The tree stood not far from the village where the series was originally devised in 1971.

> *Roam on! The light we sought is shining still.*
> *Dost thou ask proof? Our tree yet crowns the hill,*
> *Our Scholar travels yet the loved hill-side*

from 'Thyrsis'

Hope Mirrlees
Collected Poems

Edited with an introduction by
SANDEEP PARMAR

Fyfield*Books*
CARCANET

First published in Great Britain in 2011 by
Carcanet Press Limited
Alliance House
Cross Street
Manchester M2 7AQ

www.carcanet.co.uk

Paris, poems from *Moods and Tensions* and essays
copyright © the Estate of Hope Mirrlees
Previously unpublished poems and translations copyright
© the Principal and Fellows of Newnham College, Cambridge
'To Her. A twilight poem' by Jane Harrison copyright © the
Principal and Fellows of Newnham College, Cambridge

Photograph of Hope Mirrlees reproduced by permission of
the Principal and Fellows of Newnham College, Cambridge

Introduction, selection and notes copyright © Sandeep Parmar 2011
Commentary on *Paris* copyright © the Estate of Julia Briggs

The right of Sandeep Parmar to be identified as the editor
of this work has been asserted by her in accordance with
the Copyright, Designs and Patents Act of 1988
All rights reserved

A CIP catalogue record for this book is available from the British Library

ISBN 978 1 84777 075 2

The publisher acknowledges financial assistance from
Arts Council England

Typeset by XL Publishing Services, Tiverton
Printed and bound in England by SRP Ltd, Exeter

Contents

Acknowledgements	vii
Introduction	ix
A Note on the Text	xlix
Select Bibliography	lii
Hope Mirrlees, ca. 1920	liv

PARIS: A POEM (1920)	1
MOODS AND TENSIONS (1976)	
Mothers	21
The Copper-Beech in St. Giles' Churchyard	22
The Death of Cats and Roses	24
A Skull	25
Et in Arcadia Ego	26
The Land of Uz	28
The Glass Tánagra	30
The Legend of the Painted Room	30
'Une Maison Commode, Propre, et Belle. . .'	32
The Rendez-Vous	32
Bertha frightens Miss Bates	33
In a Pagan Wood	36
Sickness and Recovery at the Cape of Good Hope in Spring	37
Winter Trees	40
A Portrait of the Second Eve, Painted in Pompeian Red	43
Amor Fati	45
Heaven is Not Fairyland	45
Gulls	46
A Meditation on Donatello's Annunciation in the Church of Santa Croce, Florence	46
A Doggerel Epitaph for My Little Dog, Sally	51
Jesus Wept	52

PREVIOUSLY UNPUBLISHED POEMS AND TRANSLATIONS
  I'd like to get into your dreams   55
  Crossed in Love   55
  Love Lies Dying   56
  To Mrs Patrick Campbell   57
  To Jean, Who Loves Faerie-tales   58
  The Moon-Flowers   59
  Love   60
  Carpe Diem   61
  My Soul Was a Princess   61
  The Moon-Maid   62
  from My Mother's Pedigree   63
  The Faerie Changelings   64
  'Some talk of Alexander and some sing Monty's praise'   65
  A Friendship   66
  The Shooting Stars   66
  Ostia Antica   67
  The Toad   67
  The Invocation, by Anna de Noailles   68
  Dusk, by Albert Samain   70

ESSAYS
  Some Aspects of the Art of Alexey Mikhailovich Remizov
    (1926)   75
  Listening in to the Past (1926)   85
  An Earthly Paradise (1927)   90
  The Religion of Women (1927)   94
  Gothic Dreams (1928)   98
  Bedside Books (1928)   102

NOTES AND APPENDIX
  Abbreviations   112
  Commentary on *Paris*, by Julia Briggs   113
  Notes on the Poems and Essays   129
  Appendix: 'To Her. A twilight poem',
    by Jane Ellen Harrison   138

Index of Titles and First Lines   141

Acknowledgements

I am grateful for the assistance and support of the Principal and Fellows of Newnham College, Cambridge, for allowing me unrestricted access to the papers of Hope Mirrlees and Jane Harrison. The College's archivists, Anne Thomson and Patricia Ackerman, provided expert guidance in navigating Newnham's collections; their insights helped to shape this edition.

This edition benefits greatly from the assistance of research library staff in locating and reproducing Mirrlees-related materials: W.S. Hoole Library at the University of Alabama; the Amherst Center for Russian Culture; Special Collections, University of Glasgow; The Harry Ransom Research Center at the University of Texas, Austin; The Lilly Library, University of Indiana; the knowledgeable Mihaela Bacou and Brunhilde Biebuyck at Reid Hall (Paris); Anne Manuel at Somerville College Archives, Oxford; Special Collections, University of Cape Town Libraries; and the Victoria University Library.

For their permission, I am indebted to Hope Mirrlees's literary executors John Saunders and Margaret Ellis. Their collective wisdom and enthusiasm for this project were invaluable. I am very grateful to Judith Willson at Carcanet, who provided constant support and encouragement during every stage of this edition.

Many friends and colleagues helped at various stages of the process: Robert Ackerman, Jon Briggs, Alfred Corn, Lesley Fiedler, Rebecca Harbor, Laurence McGilvery, Sura Qadiri, Stanley Rabinowitz, Claire Saunders, Marilyn Smith and Henry Wessells. Thanks are also due to the Mirrleesian Michael Swanwick for his generosity and keen knowledge of Hope's life and work. For time, space and intellectual camaraderie, thanks must be given to Ann Pellegrini and Robert Campbell at New York University's Center for the Study of Gender and Sexuality.

I would like to express my gratitude to James Byrne – who began work on this book in the role of co-editor – for having the grace to step aside once the project hit full swing and my vision of it began to take over. This edition benefits greatly from his insight and wisdom. And finally, I am grateful to my wonderful family.

§

This edition is dedicated to the memory of Julia Briggs, whose pioneering work on *Paris* lit the torch for all future Mirrlees scholars.

Introduction

And then there is another thought. We are told now that we bear within us the seeds, not of one, but of two lives – the life of the race and the life of the individual. The life of the race makes for racial immortality; the life of the individual suffers *l'attirance de la mort*, the lure of death; and this from the outset. The unicellular animals are practically immortal; the complexity of the individual spells death. The unmarried and childless cut themselves loose from racial immortality, and are dedicated to individual life – a side track, a blind alley, yet surely a supreme end in itself.

Jane Ellen Harrison, *Reminiscences of a Student's Life* (1925)

One might expect an introduction to the poetry of Hope Mirrlees to begin with the woman herself, to offer a catalogue of biographical facts, some historical gossip, anecdotes: a fine broderie of names, dates, and places. But in the case of Hope Mirrlees, what is known about her life offers few clues about the composition of her lately rediscovered modernist 'lost masterpiece', the long poem *Paris*.[1] She rarely made reference to it in her correspondence and, soon after the Hogarth Press published *Paris* in 1920, it quickly disappeared, nearly taking with it its increasingly reclusive author. And when, reluctantly, Mirrlees returned to *Paris* fifty-two years later and excised 'blasphemous' passages before republication, the literary journal in which it appeared folded after just three issues. Rather unsettlingly, especially for scholars of modernism, Mirrlees's brilliant poem seemed like a one-off. Decades after Mirrlees's death in 1978, her poem began to re-emerge from the archives of modernist literature and has been hailed by some as an exemplary text of British modernist writing. This edition celebrates the dynamism of Mirrlees's long poem, whilst placing it within the context of her wider oeuvre, her life, and her networks of influence.

So how do we connect the woman to the work that she neglected

---

1 Julia Briggs, 'Hope Mirrlees and Continental Modernism', in *Gender in Modernism*, ed. Bonnie Kime Scott (Chicago: University of Illinois Press, 2007), p. 261.

and eventually distanced herself from? How do we explain the dramatic change in her poetics from 1920 to 1960, by which time Mirrlees had plunged into highly formal, mannered verse? How, indeed, can we reconcile the style of *Paris* with that of her later poems? This shift, seen by many as the demise of Mirrlees's literary career – she published three novels in addition to *Paris* in the 1920s and then didn't publish again for over thirty years – was linked, quite plausibly, to the death of her companion, the classics scholar Jane Harrison, in 1928. Harrison (born in 1850, and Mirrlees's elder by nearly forty years) was her tutor at Newnham College from 1910 to 1913. The two women bonded during those years and, by 1914, what Mirrlees described as a 'close friendship' with Harrison had evolved – they lived together from 1922 until the end of Jane's life. We know far more about Jane Harrison than we do about Mirrlees. Harrison was, by some accounts, the first professional female academic in Britain – in 1898 she became the first woman to give university lectures at Cambridge – and her theories on the function of ritual in ancient societies were highly influential to early twentieth-century anthropology. There have been numerous studies of her work and her involvement with the Cambridge Ritualists, and several biographies of Harrison to date. But perhaps the best-known glimpse we have of Jane Harrison is in Virginia Woolf's essay *A Room of One's Own*, delivered as two lectures at Newnham and Girton colleges the year Harrison died.

> [. . .] and then on the terrace, as if popping out to breathe the air, to glance at the garden, came a bent figure, formidable yet humble, with her great forehead and her shabby dress – could it be the famous scholar, could it be J— H— herself? All was dim, yet intense too, as if the scarf which the dusk had flung over the garden were torn asunder by star or sword – the flash of some terrible reality leaping, as its way is, out of the heart of the spring. For youth –[2]

Here Woolf is walking through the gardens of Fernham (a fictitious hybrid of Newnham and Girton) when she imagines herself back in the spring (it is actually October) and she spots Harrison's ghostly figure. The spring gives way to the 'terrible reality' of death, perhaps partly a reference to Jane's death in early April that year. Her vision of Jane, who was Woolf's friend and whose scholarship she clearly admired, appears not so coincidentally in

---

[2] Virginia Woolf, *A Room of One's Own* (1929) (London: Penguin Books, 2000), pp. 18–19.

Woolf's treatise on the lives of women writers. Famously the question of what women sacrifice, in the pursuit of intellectual life, runs throughout her essay. As Harrison wrote in her memoir:

> By what miracle I escaped marriage I do not know, for all my life long I fell in love. But, on the whole, I am glad. I do not doubt that I lost much, but I am quite sure I gained more. Marriage, for a woman at least, hampers two things that made life to me glorious – friendship and learning. In man it was always the friend, not the husband, that I wanted. Family life has never attracted me. At its best it seems to me rather narrow and selfish; at its worst, a private hell. The role of wife and mother is no easy one; with my head full of other things I might have dismally failed. On the other hand, I have a natural gift for community life. It seems to me sane and civilised and economically right. I like to live spaciously, but rather plainly, in large halls with great spaces and quiet libraries. I like to wake in the morning with the sense of a great, silent garden around me.'[3]

Women must, as readers and authors, preserve the community; they must choose friendship and learning over the more mundane options of marriage and family; they must be prepared to see the ghosts of their literary mothers coming out for air on an imaginary spring evening. And this is where we turn again to Hope. When Jane died, Mirrlees's life changed irrevocably. After Harrison's funeral, Hope spent a few weeks in France to recover from the strain of nursing Jane during her final months. She dreaded returning to England to face her and Jane's mutual friends.[4] She held onto one line from a letter of condolence as the most consoling of all, one she would paraphrase many years later to T.S. Eliot's widow, her dear friend Valerie: 'Anyhow, what a comfort for you to have been all you were to her.'[5] It was from Virginia Woolf.

3   Jane Harrison, *Reminiscences of a Student's Life* (London: Hogarth Press, 1925), p. 88.
4   Hope Mirrlees wrote in a letter to Mary MacCarthy dated 6 June 1928: 'I am coming back next week and you are practically the only person I want to see. There are many others I must see – both business and ordinary kindness demand it. If Jane's old friends want to be kind to me and to talk about her I must let them.' Mary MacCarthy Papers, Courtesy, The Lilly Library, Indiana University, Bloomington, Indiana.
5   Letter from Virginia and Leonard Woolf to Hope Mirrlees, 17 April 1928, Hope Mirrlees Papers, Series III, Box I, Special Collections, University of Maryland Libraries. According to Hermione Lee's biogaphy, *Virginia Woolf* (London: Chatto and Windus, 1996), p. 574, Mirrlees's paraphrase of Woolf's statement was 'But remember what you have had.'

§

Helen Hope Mirrlees was born on 8 April 1887 in Chislehurst, Kent and died in 1978, at the age of ninety-one. She was educated at St Leonard's School in St Andrews and, later, after a year-long stint studying at the Royal Academy of Dramatic Art, took up classics at Newnham from 1910 to 1913 (she did not sit the Tripos examinations). Mirrlees's mother, Emily Lina Mirrlees, was descended from Scottish aristocracy, the Moncrieffs, and her father, William Julius Mirrlees, was an engineer in Glasgow. W.J. Mirrlees co-founded the Mirrlees-Tongaat (now Tongaat-Hulett) Company based in Natal, a lucrative South African sugar manufacturer. As an heiress to the Mirrlees-Tongaat fortunes, Hope spent much of her life in relative comfort as an exile from Britain, living in South Africa and France and making extended stays in southern Europe. The Mirrlees family – which also included Hope's two younger siblings, William Henry Buchanan (Reay) and Margaret Rosalys (Margot) – was, it would seem, close, convivial and eccentric. Pet names pepper their correspondence to each other: 'Sneezor'; 'Bolo'; 'Snowdrop'; 'Skip'; 'Mappie'; 'Nursey'; 'Hubbie'; 'Wifey'; 'Silly Sealie'; 'Seal-Child Mirrlees' and more. The letters from Hope to her mother Lina (referred to as either 'Mappie' or 'The Seal' by her children) keep track of the intimate details of Hope's daily life whilst she was away intermittently in France between 1913 and 1926.[6] Hope often consulted her parents about housing and travel, in part because she relied on their continuous financial support. But one also senses that Hope's connection with her mother was, until Lina's death in 1948, a crucial and substantial anchor to her own identity as a Moncrieff and as a member of an aristocratic set. This is not the least because Lina herself figures in the lives and memoirs of some of Hope's most auspicious associations, including T.S. Eliot, the poet and critic Fredegond Shove, the Strachey family and, of course, Jane Harrison. In the Hope Mirrlees archive, a long, unpublished typescript, entitled 'A Discursive and Selective Pedigree of Emily Lina Mirrlees, Née Moncrieff, By Her Daughter, Hope Mirrlees', attempts to trace the Moncrieff lineage through her maternal ancestry.[7] It is an intricate web extending back several centuries through baronets and Scottish royalty

---

6 Details of Hope Mirrlees's family correspondence are in Hope Mirrlees Papers, Newnham College Archives, Cambridge, 2/1.

7 The typescript of this family history and its associated notes are located in Hope Mirrlees Papers, Newnham College Archives, Cambridge, 4/2/2.

(including both the Lyons and the Lindsays). In it Hope claimed that Lina had 'inherited her mother's beauty, her father's charm, and the high courage of her ancestors'. Lina was evidently very fond of poetry, and counted Wordsworth as her favourite, followed closely by Robert Browning and Dante Gabriel Rossetti (whose poems she could recite from memory). The Mirrlees family's closeness – and Hope's financial dependence – meant that she frequently returned to stay at the family home between 1913 and 1948; first at Cranmer Road in Cambridge and Mount Blow near Great Shelford and then later at Shamley Wood, or 'The Shambles', near Guildford, Surrey. Hope's recollections conjure images of witty 'table talk', extravagance and good-natured teasing by all – the warmth of the Mirrlees family was not lost on its most famous boarder, Tom Eliot. Eliot, who lived with the Mirrleeses during World War II, wrote to Hope in 1951 that Shamley was the nearest thing to home he had had since his childhood and 'it may be that I did there what will be regarded as my best work', a reference to his *Four Quartets*. About his devotion to Hope's mother, he wrote: 'I think of Mappie for a moment every day – as you say, in eternity'.[8] Eliot had been, for a time, part of the family circle.

Hope Mirrlees figures in the biographies of her contemporaries as a stunningly beautiful woman, a fierce intellectual and a peripheral Bloomsbury figure. In the 1920s she appears in the correspondence and memoirs of Virginia and Leonard Woolf, Lytton Strachey, Dora Carrington, Roger Fry and Mary MacCarthy, and she was chosen as one of the literary executors for the Bloomsbury hostess, Lady Ottoline Morrell. (However, Hope's correspondence with another of Morrell's executors, Robert Gathorne-Hardy, reveals that trustees of the estate, especially Morrell's family, ultimately blocked her involvement.) Whilst at Newnham, Mirrlees's studies were carefully supervised by Harrison, who wrote letters to Hope's mother and also visited Cranmer Road on occasion. Harrison wrote to both Lina and Hope in the summer of 1910 expressing her relief that an engagement between Hope and an unnamed man had been broken off. Judging from the tenor of these letters, Harrison doubted that Hope had found a suitable match, feeling that her 'hour has not struck'.[9] Jane wrote that she was looking forward to Hope's return to Cambridge

---

8 T.S. Eliot to Hope Mirrlees, 8 July 1951, Papers of Hope Mirrlees, Series I, Box I, University of Maryland Archives.
9 Jane Harrison to Emily Lina Mirrlees, Hope Mirrlees Papers, Newnham College Archives, Cambridge, 1/1/2.

INTRODUCTION xiii

the following term. As it turns out, the man to whom Harrison refers was almost certainly the illustrator and painter Henry Justice Ford (1860–1941). Three letters from Ford – two addressed to Hope and one to her parents – reveal that Ford was indeed courting Hope and had visited the Mirrlees family in 1910. Ford was born in London and won a scholarship to attend Clare College, Cambridge, where he gained a First degree in classics. He later studied art at the Slade under the tuition of Alphonse Legros and fought as part of the Artists Rifles regiment during World War I. His most famous illustrations were for Andrew Lang's hugely popular series of twelve Fairy Books for children, which Hope would certainly have read during her youth. Hope and Ford shared some common acquaintances in London – Ford ran with the likes of J.M. Barrie and Arthur Conan Doyle – but, while it is impossible to say for certain, it is likely the two met through Mary MacCarthy, who wrote glowingly of meeting Ford in a letter to Hope. A lovesick Ford wrote to Mirrlees from London's Saville Club in 1910, just before the funeral of King Edward:

> I was so very sad and miserable all this afternoon that I had to come up here for human companionship. It is so horrid to be 60 miles away from you after being so close for two days. But I've cheered up a little playing billiards with some jolly fellows and so I can write a little letter and feel happy talking to you again darling thing. What a happy little time it was. Did you like it? I just look forward to next Sunday and in the meanwhile shall busily ply the drawings like till there are very few left to do. [. . .] I think your dear father and mother are the sweetest kindest creatures in the world. They *have* been good to me, bless them. I think they must hate me coming and disturbing their peace so, and they are so nice about it. I don't quite know how to thank them because there is nothing to say adequate. Dear pet are you happy? And tell me if you enjoyed seeing me. [. . .]
>
>   Good night beloved. I send you a million kisses (and they 'seem too few' for me)
>   Henry

It is delicious hot and stuffy but it makes me rather a sleepy dog – but it is one that is not so sleepy to want his cat *very badly* tonight.[10]

---

10 Henry Justice Ford to Hope Mirrlees, Hope Mirrlees Papers, Newnham College Archives, Cambridge, 2/1/2.

From what little is in these letters, one comes away feeling that Ford is a frivolous character who pours his childish affections into unwilling hands. Perhaps Hope's letters to Ford (which haven't surfaced) would prove otherwise. But it hardly seems possible that these letters were written by a man of fifty, and considering that Hope was only twenty-three years old at the time, one may be able to see why the engagement dissolved. As for Jane's letters to Hope and Lina, some of Jane's biographers have read in them the concerned voice of a tutor, others may wish to find in them evidence of Jane's attraction to and possessiveness of Hope. All of this centres on the question of whether or not the two women had entered into a romantic relationship – either in 1910 or later – a question that many of Harrison's biographers have attempted to answer and others have skilfully avoided. While it may not be relevant to Harrison's work, I would contend that inquiries into Hope's writing that take sexuality into account deepen our understanding of the texts – especially her fiction. Therefore the nature of Harrison and Mirrlees's relationship *is* relevant to Hope's writing, not merely because the two women exchanged ideas and worked very closely on collaborative projects after Mirrlees left Newnham, but because of the intimately coded (and hence necessarily evasive) private intellectual life they subsequently shared. In a way that was not unlike the Mirrlees custom of family names, Jane and Hope referred to each other as 'Elder' and 'Younger' Wife or Walrus ('EW' or 'YW') in their letters. During Jane's early days teaching at Newnham, three female students gave her a toy stuffed bear, which Jane named 'OO', short for 'The Old One'. The Bear dwelled in the 'Cave' (Jane's room) and had a totemic significance for Hope and Jane – he negotiated meetings between his 'younger' and 'elder' wife, and in part embodied their not only unconventional but impossible union by providing the 'male' aspect of a secret, fantasy marriage. A previously unpublished poem written by Harrison for Hope in 1921, entitled 'To Her. A twilight poem', makes reference to the Bear's place as both women's husband: 'My husband chose her out / To be his concubine / His morganatic wife / And last – O joy divine / We dwell together free from strife / His younger and his elder wife.'[11]

The poem ends with the elder wife's anxiety over separation and mortality; its 'twilight' is Harrison's own advanced age and she

---

11 This poem is in manuscript in Hope Mirrlees Papers, Newnham College Archives, Cambridge, 1/4/3. The entire poem is published in this edition.

offers a suggestive, half-lit obscurity of personal detail (Jane suggests that Hope is part Jewish, makes mention of their study of Russian in Paris and also references Hope's first novel *Madeleine: One of Love's Jansenists*).[12] 'Morganatic', used to describe a (often polygamous) marriage entered into with a woman of lower standing, characterises the Bear's superiority to Hope. The sign of the Great Bear, the constellation Ursa Major, also appears in their correspondence and, most significantly, at the end of Mirrlees's *Paris*. And although Jane's 'poem' isn't a serious attempt at the form (she also wrote some cringe-worthy limericks for Hope), the paradigm of their relationship is laid out and the power structure that underlies it is clear: Jane and the 'OO' watch over the younger 'concubine' Mirrlees and she is a source of 'joy divine', companionship and amusement for the Bear and the Elder Wife. The Bear also had a special, additional meaning for Jane dating back to a research visit she made to the Acropolis years before she met Hope. In her memoir, *Reminiscences of a Student's Life*, Harrison writes:

> The first time I went to Athens I had the luck to make a small archaeological discovery. I was turning over the fragments in the Acropolis Museum, then little more than a lumber-room. In a rubbish pile in the corner, to my great happiness, I lighted on a small stone figure of a bear. The furry hind paw was sticking out and caught my eye. I immediately had her – it was manifestly a she bear – brought out and honourably placed. She must have been set up originally in the precinct of Artemis Brauronia. Within this precinct, year by year, went on the *arkteia* or bear-service. No well-born Athenian would marry a girl unless she had accomplished her *bear-service*, unless she was in a word, *confirmed* to Artemis.[13]

Here the small stone figure of the 'she bear', essential to the maturation rites of Athenian women, takes on a symbolic importance: without her girls cannot become women nor can they be brought into the community through marriage. At the end of her life, Harrison wrote that she would have liked to have 'founded a learned community for women, with vows of consecration and a

---

12 It is possible that Hope was partly of Jewish descent through her paternal grandmother, James Buchanan Mirrlees's second wife Helen Eliza Gumprecht. Gumprecht is a surname found in Poland, Hungary and Germany between the fifteenth and nineteenth centuries among Ashkenazic Jews. The connection, albeit a distant one, was a subject of discussion in the Mirrlees family.
13 Harrison, *Reminiscences*, pp. 70–71.

beautiful rule and habit'. In some ways this was achieved through her life with Hope and certainly during her years at Newnham. These types of 'vows' or initiation rites in the Greek tradition were central to Harrison's ideas about the essence of art, religion, and indeed drama:

> I have elsewhere tried to show that Art is not the handmaid of Religion, but that Art in some sense springs out of Religion, and that between them is a connecting link, a bridge, and that bridge is Ritual. On that bridge, emotionally, I halt. It satisfies something within me that is appeased by neither Religion nor Art. A ritual dance, a ritual procession with vestments and lights and banners, move me as no sermon, no hymn, no picture, no poem has ever moved me; perhaps it is because a procession seems to me like life, like *durée* itself, caught and fixed before me.[14]

Ritual is the bridge extending into a forgotten past, and the space in which it can be experienced and re-experienced, an idea owing to Bergson's concept of duration. The influence of Harrison's ideas about ritual and religion on Hope's novels has been the subject of scholarly enquiry, not the least because her most famous novel, *Lud-in-the-Mist* (1926) begins with an epigraph taken from Harrison's *Prolegomena to the Study of Greek Religion* (1903). However, what is of greater interest, in this edition, is the presence of ritual in Mirrlees's poetry, both before and after Jane's death. Mirrlees herself reflected on the two women's mutual influence whilst attempting to write Jane's biography in the early 1930s:

> Influence was hardly the word of [Jane's] effect on me. It was, rather, re-creation. All the same, I know that I did have a great influence on her – she told me so. It was after we came back from Spain, she said to me that she had learned a great deal from me; from the way I attacked the whole of a civilisation, instead of just a part of it.[15]

It is clear that Hope believed in this 're-creation', but how this might have been altered by Jane's death is not as apparent. Did she carry on, as before, doing in her work what Jane supposedly admired her for, that is, attacking 'the whole of a civilisation'? If Jane's 'attack' was on religion or moralising theology, for instance, then how was Mirrlees's revolutionary vision so total, so complete?

14 Harrison, *Reminiscences*, p. 84.
15 Jane Harrison Collection, Newnham College Archives, Cambridge, 4/3/1.

It is hard to imagine. Mirrlees's work, especially her novels, almost always entwines itself into the net of civilising forces: religion, cultural history, tradition, family. Her criticism is made from within, but in no way does it discredit these forces on a wider scale; generally speaking, her attack leaves intact some of the values one would expect Harrison to have railed against. More importantly, Mirrlees's later poetry published in the 1960s is highly reverential of a cultural – particularly British, sometimes Catholic – past that only makes very light mockery of tradition (in one instance the hallowed halls of Oxbridge, where she imagines herself as an outsider). But before we consider Hope's poetry in depth it is crucial to give an account of the years after she left Newnham and the time she spent living and studying in Paris.

It is almost possible to reconstruct loosely the years from 1913 to 1928 through surviving letters from Jane to Hope. In 1912 Jane wrote from Italy whilst she was en route to the Temple of Thermopylae to Hope, who was in Cambridge; in October 1913 Hope sojourned in Paris with Karin Costelloe (an early psychoanalyst who would later marry Virginia Woolf's brother, Adrian) and the two women were introduced to Parisian literary society. We learn from a friend of Hope's that she and Karin were invited to dine at the home of the poet Anna de Noailles, that they visited the English writer Mary Robinson (also known as Madame Duclaux) and that they lunched with Edith Wharton. (Wharton apparently snubbed them, and the two girls privately dubbed her 'Old Warts'.) Jane visited her in April 1914 and then again in June. From 1915 onwards Hope wrote in her unfinished biography of Jane that '[Jane] gets a new lease of life from the joy of the discovery of Russian and Russia', and we know that her study of Russian began in Paris that year. The two women spent 1918 almost entirely in Paris studying languages at the École des Langues Orientales. In the spring of 1919, Hope finished *Paris: A Poem* (1920) while presumably completing her first novel, *Madeleine: One of Love's Jansenists*, which was the product of many years' work. During the first months of 1920, on a visit to Seville, Hope became afflicted with (at least from Jane's report) typhoid fever and Hope's parents were summoned. Once Hope had recovered, they both motored through Spain. Jane threw herself into learning Spanish and discovered a passion for the paintings of El Greco through the writings of Maurice Barrès.

It wasn't until 1922 that Jane, having left her career and community behind at Newnham, burned her personal papers and went to live with Hope in Paris on a more permanent basis. According to Hope, her family required her to have a chaperone if she wished to settle in Paris and Jane was happy to oblige. Although Jane was ageing, and her health was failing – whilst in Paris, Harrison was under the care of a physician named Moutier in whom she (perhaps unwisely) invested a great deal of faith – the two women were able to carry on their lives together in Paris, as foreign women travelling and studying, in a way that would have been more noticeable in London. Before Virginia Woolf (known for her occasionally savagely formed opinions of people) went to visit the two women in Paris she wrote in a letter to Mary MacCarthy they had a 'Sapphic flat somewhere'[16] and had earlier complained to Clive Bell that Hope's novel *Madeleine* was 'all Sapphism so far as I've got – Jane and herself'.[17] But whether or not Harrison and Mirrlees's relationship was sexual (and Mirrlees herself claimed, coyly, that she wasn't a 'Sapphist in the strictest sense') Paris allowed the two women a certain degree of freedom in a more liberal environment. Initially, Hope and Jane travelled through the French countryside – they went to Nancy to attend sessions on 'optimistic autosuggestion' by the psychologist Émile Coué and explored Burgundy. Both women appear to have taken Coué's practices seriously – especially Jane, who wrote to Hope (during a brief period apart) that she had 'Coué'd' for two hours in an attempt to ward off loneliness.[18] The Hôtel de Londres on the rue Bonaparte (in the 6ème arrondissement) was their first home together in Paris, but they soon had to move on, finding it unsatisfactory, in part because they could not take meals in their rooms. Through Bertrand Russell's first wife, Alys, Jane and Hope managed to find more spacious and comfortable lodgings in the American University Women's Club on the rue de Chevreuse in Montparnasse, where they lived from 1922 to 1925. The Club, founded by the wealthy American philanthropist Elizabeth Mills Reid in the first decades of the twentieth century, was established as a residence in 1922 for American postgraduate women in Paris. All of the comforts of American life

---

16 Woolf letter to Mary MacCarthy, 22 April 1923, in *The Letters of Virginia Woolf*, Vol. III, ed. Nigel Nicolson (London: Hogarth Press, 1977), p. 30. This published version of the letter omits the reference to Sapphism but other sources, including the original archived letter, confirm that this is the omitted phrase.
17 Woolf letter to Clive Bell, 24 September 1919, in *The Letters of Virginia Woolf*, Vol. II, p. 391.
18 Harrison to Hope Mirrlees, April 1922, Jane Harrison Collection, Newnham College Archives, Cambridge, 1/3/4.

could be found there – 'admirable cooking of the best French kind (touched by American)' – and the company of American women was at once irritating and comforting for Hope. She wrote to her mother that the Club was so desperate to have Jane as a resident that they offered her a sitting room free of charge if she would agree to stay.[19] An article Hope wrote in 1927 for *Time & Tide* (reproduced in this edition) entitled 'An Earthly Paradise' contrasts their life in the substandard Hôtel de Londres with their experience at the rue de Chevreuse:

> Fortunately for the weak and helpless there are many substitutes for the 'Friend behind phenomena' – good servants, for instance, kind aunts, a large balance at the bank. So if one is to realise adequately the horrors of the atheist's universe, it is necessary for a period to be cut off from these kindly sources of comfort ... abroad, say, in a little unfriendly hotel, managed by people as impersonal as the *chauffage central*, and as cold; where everything even a daily bath, is made as difficult as human, or rather, as devilish ingenuity can compass, so that a few innocent cases of books make one feel as guilty and as helpless as a murderer seeking for a hiding-place for the remains of his victim; and whence one is driven daily, whatever the weather, to seek like Lear, as a witty friend most feelingly put it, one's omelette in the storm.[20]

In August of 1923 and 1924, Jane and Hope left Paris for the Abbaye de Pontigny in Burgundy, where the philosopher Paul Desjardins (with the assistance of Charles Du Bos) hosted the yearly Décades de Pontigny, which ran regularly from 1910 to 1940 and halted only during World War I. These *décades* lasted for ten days, with *entretiens*, or symposia, set around a literary, philosophical or religious question during the afternoons. The attendees were intellectuals, mostly from Europe or Britain – André Gide, Jacques Rivière, André Maurois, Paul Valéry, Jean Tardieu, Heinrich Mann and

---

19 Minutes from board meetings at the American University Women's Club confirm that because of Harrison's scholarly reputation she was offered a studio for use as a sitting room free of charge and paid a 'reduced rate' for her bedroom. The minutes also state that Mirrlees, 'the friend who is travelling with her', would pay the full standard rate.
20 Hope would have heard the phrase 'Friend behind Phenomena' from Jane Harrison's friend, Gilbert Murray. Murray paraphrases Edwyn Bevan's coinage of 'great Friend behind the Universe' in his 'Stoicism and Sceptics' lectures. See letter from Jane Harrison to Gilbert Murray, 30 July 1921, in *Jane Ellen Harrison: A Portrait from Letters*, ed. Jessie Stewart (London: Merlin Press, 1959), p. 182.

Lytton Strachey were among those invited – and the meetings were held in a Cistercian abbey bought by Desjardins. Jane wrote a glowing letter to Gilbert Murray about the 1923 *décades* in which she described Pontigny as 'an amazing place' with 'perfectly managed' *entretiens*.[21] But in an undated letter to her mother, Hope wrote that she was utterly bored at Pontigny, and she remarked during a group gathering (presumably with dismissive sarcasm) 'Moi je n'ai pas de vie intérieure!' which, according to one of Jane's biographers Annabel Robinson, 'staggered the French'.[22] Lytton Strachey wrote to Dora Carrington the same year about being at Pontigny, to which Carrington replied that she was 'delighted to be spared such tortures' as the *entretiens*.

> But WHAT FIENDS! Mania, is too mild a word for deliberate torture. How can you discuss translation for ten afternoons from half past two until half past four? It just shows what the Frogs are to choose the dullest and stoggiest, the most unsympathetic hours of the day to try and shine in intelligence. I *should* make a speech if I was you. But not on translation. I should make a speech on 'Imbecility in the Lower Animals, the Frogs' in the style of Swift, (or perhaps Strachey). I should give the habits of the toads and frogs who congregated in an Abbaye. Mercifully I am spared my speech!

In the same letter she also urges Strachey to get close to Hope and Jane: 'I think the Jane-Hope liaison interests me most. Win their confidences. I am sure they are a fascinating couple. [Boris] Anrep once gave me such an interesting account of them.'[23]

Whether or not Hope enjoyed Pontigny is debatable. Years later, when recollecting these years for Jane's biography, Hope wrote that she and Jane made 'delightful friends' there, but this may have been an intentional misremembering. What is more interesting is how the discussion about translation may have affected Hope's own work and the course of the following years. In 1924, Hope and Jane jointly began two works of translation from Russian, to be completed over the next three years: *The Life of the Archpriest*

---

21 Letter from Jane Harrison to Gilbert Murray, 29 August 1923, in Stewart, pp. 191–2.
22 Annabel Robinson, *The Life and Work of Jane Ellen Harrison* (Oxford: Oxford University Press, 2002), p. 294.
23 Letter from Dora Carrington to Lytton Strachey, 27 August 1923, in *Carrington: Letters and Extracts from Her Diaries*, ed. David Garnett (London: Jonathan Cape, 1970), p. 258.

Avvakum by Himself (1924) and, a further indulgence on the figure of the bear, *The Book of the Bear* (1926), twenty-one folk-tales. Robinson tells us that the theme of the *décades* of 1923 was 'Y-at-il dans la poésie d'un people un trésor réservé, impenetrable aux étrangers?' and that this topic broke down into more specific debates about the role of the poet and translator (who, therefore, begets a new audience for the poet) in different languages, cultures and nations. Jane's affinity for all things Russian is well documented, most of all in Harrison's own memoir. But the level at which Hope and Jane collaborated on these projects is difficult to decipher: there are no surviving manuscripts or notes for either book. We do know that during 1923 Hope completed her novel *The Counterplot* (1924) and that on 20 April 1924 she began writing what would become *Lud-in-the-Mist* (1926).[24] In a letter to her mother she writes:

> I began a new book on Sunday – the subtitle of which will possibly be A Story of <u>Smuggling, Kidnapping and Adventures on the Borders of Fairyland (This is a secret!!!)</u> It went swimmingly for three days and I wrote away at a great pace and then I stuck – as I knew nothing whatever about smugglers and hadn't a background for the countryside. So I must get some books about smugglers and merchants and things.[25]

As for their collaborations in Russian – it seems unlikely that Hope was involved at any length in the translation of *Avvakum*. Jane didn't receive the Russian manuscript until sometime after mid-May 1924 and by mid-June Hope was in London, staying with her mother near Hyde Park. But Jane and Hope had seen the manuscript – friends of theirs, the Russian émigré writer Alexei Remizov (1877-1957) and his wife Seraphima, owned a copy – and they had read it aloud at the Remizovs' home.[26] A July letter from Jane to

---

[24] In a letter from Jane Harrison to Jessie Stewart, dated 24 Jan 1923, Harrison writes: 'Hope is buried in her new book. She is writing it a second time ... Her patience amazes me she says she must write it a third time to get the surface right.' Within days Hope's father died unexpectedly whilst on a trip to Buenos Aires. On 20 February 1923, Hope returned to London. Jane Harrison Collection, Newnham College Archives, Cambridge, 1/4/7.

[25] Mirrlees's letter to her mother, 24 April 1924, Hope Mirrlees Papers, Newnham College Archives, Cambridge, 2/1/3.

[26] Mirrlees's letter to her mother in May 1924 reads: 'We want to translate a wonderful Russian classic of the 17th Century – the autobiography of the Protopope Avvakum. [...] As it's in Old Russian it's very difficult for us to read, and besides we have not yet succeeded in getting a copy, so the Remizovs are

D.S. Mirsky, the Russian critic and historian who had suggested translating *Avvakum* to Jane and procured the manuscript, suggests that while Hope was away, she and Mirsky would finish the book. The two met in Paris at the rue de Chevreuse to discuss the book and Mirsky wrote the preface. The speed at which Jane accomplished the translation of this seventeenth-century Old Russian text is remarkable – but modern translators have criticised her edition for its use of archaism (in effect, it appears that Jane pitched the language rather higher than the colloquial original). It is much more likely that Mirrlees and Harrison collaborated on *The Book of the Bear*, which Hope would have been translating whilst writing *Lud-in-the-Mist*. As the fantasy writer Michael Swanwick points out in his study of Mirrlees's life and work, the influence of Alexei Remizov, a modernist writer of an almost Gothic sensibility, is visibile in her novel. Remizov, who was also a painter, was the subject of an article by Mirrlees published in a 1926 issue of *Le Journal de Psychologie Normale et Pathologique* (reproduced in this edition). Remizov was the only living contributor to *The Book of the Bear* and certainly Mirrlees and Harrison's decision to place the living folklorist alongside older (often anonymous) ones actively brings folklore into the present. In their introduction, they argue that Remizov 'has evolved his elaborate style and intensely individual fantasy from the simple rhythms of Russian folk-tales' and Remizov himself is described as an almost fairy creature, hoarding mysterious painted toys in his Paris flat. Putting aside some of the homogenising cultural myth about Russians that shape the introduction – and indeed the whole book, Russians are 'Bears' after all – we can imagine that Remizov's example of making-new older 'simple rhythms' inspired Hope to develop her own 'intensely individual fantasy' in *Lud*. Swanwick, a well-informed reader of Mirrlees's fantasy novel, suggests that Remizov 'freed [Hope] from the strictures of realism' and that fantasy provided a more successful mode of writing for the kinds of social critique (in the

> reading it with us. Today was our second lesson. A young man called Dixon was there – half English and half Russian – and he was a great help in explaining. He is going to translate the Remizov book I told you about last time – we have promised to touch it up, as his English is not as good as his Russian. So perhaps you will soon be able to read it.' Mirrlees is most likely referring to the Russian-American writer and publisher Vladimir Dixon (1900–29), who was known to the Paris Russian émigré community and was an ardent admirer of Remizov's writing. It is unclear whether Dixon was involved in subsequent translation attempts. Hope Mirrlees Papers, Newnham College Archives, Cambridge, 2/1/3.

form of highly staged *roman à clef*) that formed the basis of Mirrlees's previous two novels.[27] Both *Madeleine* and *The Counterplot* are thinly (albeit ornately) disguised projections of Hope's own family drama. *Lud-in-the-Mist* breaks from Hope's rewriting of her own life and her being what Virginia Woolf described as 'her own heroine – capricious, exacting, exquisite, learned and beautifully dressed'.[28] In 1927, Newnham College's magazine, *Thersites*, printed a review of *Lud*:

> Misled by the notice of a fraudulent bookseller, I positively bought 'Lud in the Mist', thinking it to be a novel about Newnham. I think it worth mentioning this, because, terrible as were my rage and mortification on finding that the book was really a fairy story with a profound moral and psychological significance, they were insensibly charmed away by paragraph after paragraph of Miss Mirrlees's spell. Personally I can never understand allegories, but I do not think this one spoils the story any more than that of Gulliver or the Faery Queen; the creation of Lud in the Mist, the town that has the unearthly glow of 16th century Flemish pictures and the ageless enchantment of a fairy tale, is so powerful that fantastic, mannered, as it is, one accepts it as 'quite true'. To say that such things really are, and to make us believe it is to perform a very astonishing feat.
>
> In Miss Mirrlees's last novel 'The Counterplot', one detected a curious individual flavour, more subtly and completely individual than that of any modern writer I remember to have read. It is not accounted for by her conception of character or her approach to realism, and yet it informs both these; its tangible expression is, I think, her style, which in its elaborate yet clear-cut and deeply coloured nature suggests a series of pictures in mosaic. The inward feeling it gives is of a bitter sweet taste left upon the tongue, or of one of those scents, harsh and infinitely strange which one sometimes smells in filigree bottles in a curiosity shop. In one sense, 'Lud in the Mist' is a more suitable ground for Miss Mirrlees than a modern story; to my mind the drawback to the 'Counterplot' was that all-embracing pedantry, extending to every walk of life from the mediaeval Spanish convent to the naval smoke-room. One wearied of being told so

---

27 Michael Swanwick, *Hope-in-the-Mist: The Extraordinary Career & Mysterious Life of Hope Mirrlees* (New Jersey: Temporary Culture, 2009), p. 32.
28 Woolf, letter to Lady Cecil, 1 September 1925, in *The Letters of Virginia Woolf*, Vol. III, pp. 200–1.

much and so often what one either knew, or, not knowing, did not wish to know. About fairies, however, she cannot tell us too much: she must in fact, tell us everything as we go on, and leave nothing out. And what intimate revelations she makes to us of the intangible, the lovely and the strange![29]

Certainly, one can extend this estimation of Mirrlees's hyper-real style, which 'suggests a series of pictures in mosaic', to that of her poem *Paris*. According to Jane Harrison, Hope felt that Paris was 'the end of her soul' and it is clear that the city fuelled her literary aspirations.[30] One imagines that – by sheer proximity – she was lured towards the iconoclasm of French language poets like Mallarmé, Reverdy, Cendrars, Apollinaire and Cocteau. Their influence – the visual and sonic layering, the use of white space, caesurae and a unique typeface, the interest in psychological time and the pervasive concept of *durée* – is certainly evident when one reads *Paris*. Mirrlees was exposed to the rapidly changing aesthetics on the French art scene – she was friends with Gertrude Stein and the painter Marie Blanchard – and through a connection of Roger Fry's she was admitted to Auguste Pellerin's monomaniacal private collection of Cézannes in the wealthy Neuilly district of Paris.

Harrison and Mirrlees stayed in Paris until Harrison's health declined more seriously.[31] On 30 September 1925, the two women left the American Women's Club and wintered in the Midi, after what Jane described as 'three strenuous years of Paris life'.[32] In the spring of 1926 they returned to London and stayed for a few weeks

29 *Thersites*, Lent Term, no. 82, 'Lud in the Mist', review by 'J.'. Newnham College Archives, Cambridge.
30 Hope was apparently keen for Katherine Mansfield to review *Madeleine* in 1919, but Mansfield confided in a letter to her husband, John Middleton Murray dated 18 October 1919: 'I do not like Virginia's woman; she is as clever as you like but frightfully pretentious & precious and like a foreigner who knows her Paris – *from within*. But it's an interesting book to review.' Mansfield did not review it, but her discomfort with Mirrlees's familiarity with Paris is not unlike Woolf's own sense that Mirrlees's affinity for Parisian life and culture was somehow unnatural, irresponsible and pretentious. See *The Collected Letters of Katherine Mansfield, Volume III 1919–1920*, ed. Vincent O'Sullivan and Margaret Scott (Oxford: Clarendon Press, 1993), pp. 31–3.
31 Hope Mirrlees letter to Suzanne Henig, private collection, n.d.
32 Letter from Jane Harrison to Jessie Stewart, 16 September 1925. Jane Harrison Collection, Newnham College Archives, Cambridge, 1/4/8. A letter dated 23 April 1925 from the Club's Dean, Virginia Gildersleeve, states that after her departure Harrison would be made an honorary lifetime member of the American University Women's Club.

in a maisonette on Weymouth Street before taking a lease on 11 Mecklenburgh Street, on the edge of Bloomsbury near the Gray's Inn Road. In her notes for Jane's biography, Hope describes the elder woman's rapid mental and physical decline. We get a glimpse of a woman much reduced not only by age and sickness but also by her inability to develop her years of scholarship further.[33] With the proceeds of *The Book of the Bear*, Hope and Jane rented the house of the eccentric novelist and suffragist Alice Dew-Smith in Rye for the summer. Because of a thrombosis, Jane was rushed back to London in an ambulance where she died of leukaemia on 15 April 1928.

After Jane's death, Hope's life becomes much less documented in the letters and memoirs of her contemporaries. Her remaining correspondents trail off in the 1940s. We know that in May 1928, Hope stayed with the writer Margaret Behrens – a mutual friend of hers and Jane's – at Behrens's home in Menton, a resort town on the Franco-Italian border long renowned for its health benefits. In 1929 she converted to Catholicism and settled in Kensington. As with everything she undertook, Hope devoted hours of scholarship to understanding Catholic doctrine. Although she was baptised Catholic soon after birth – in accordance with the religion of her father's family – Hope had always 'kicked against' it, much like her parents who explored various religions before settling on Christian Science in the 1920s. Mirrlees's archive holds an embossed certificate of acceptance from the Vatican, dated 29 December 1933. She records conversations with her priests and sermons, often warnings against sin, in her notebooks.

> Sanctity – [Father Thurston] assured me that by just living an ordinary life and even by just being moderately faithful one was quite safe to go to Heaven.
> [...]
> Good Resolutions – To accept my talent gratefully and to offer it to God. To pray that if it never gets recognition that I may accept it with resignation; and that if it does, I may accept it with humility.

A uniform picture emerges from Hope's correspondence and notebooks in the 1930s. Hope's religious devotion is coupled with a fear of condemnation, of death and, above all, of sin. She writes in 1935:

---

33 Hope Mirrlees's notes for her unfinished biography of Jane Harrison can be found in the Jane Harrison Collection, Newnham College Archives, Cambridge, 4/3/1.

> What [Father] Connor said to me:
> It is just when things seem at their very worst, when the bottom seems knocked out of everything, it is just <u>then</u>, that something quite unforeseeable happens that puts the bottom back again. What our religion gives us is not the certainty of things coming right, but what is called in the world <u>guts</u>, to carry on – <u>that</u> is assured us.[34]

Undoubtedly, Hope's conversion gave her a certain degree of solace or at least a sense of continuity that may have been lacking in the wake of Jane's death. By 1929, Virginia Woolf points out to a mutual friend that Hope has lost her looks and grown fat, thereby implying that Jane's death had, at least physically, changed her. In photographs, Hope appears at Ottoline Morrell's Gower Street home alongside W.B. Yeats and Walter de la Mare. The figure of Mirrlees seated in Morrell's garden in 1936 is staid and older; by this time she hadn't published for ten years. Her considerable correspondence with Morrell tells us little of real substance; we know Hope took up photography at Ottoline's encouragement in the 1930s and that in 1936 she moved out of London to Surrey and stayed with her mother during the war.

After a visit to Jessie Stewart's home in May 1932, Jessie and Hope hatched a plan to write a biography of Jane. Any visitor to the Jane Harrison archive at Newnham soon becomes aware that these papers are the record of a frustrated and failed attempt. Animosity colours the letters between Jessie and Hope – Jessie was a favoured pupil and friend of Jane's, but Hope held the supreme position and was a difficult and reluctant biographer. Stewart would, many years later, bring out a portrait of Jane's life in letters written to Gilbert Murray, but it was far from the original vision of the project. Hope simply could not bring herself to write an account of Jane's years following her departure from Cambridge. By 1943, she had soured on the idea and wrote in a letter to Jessie:

> [T]he problem of what to say and what to leave out is a very difficult one. And my inability to solve it is one of my principal reasons for wishing to abdicate. Jane was extremely reserved about her own past. She had weathered a great many storms, and I think wanted them to be forgotten – in fact, I feel almost certain that she did. And yet if one omits them, the life loses what

---

[34] The notebooks from which these quotations are taken can be found in Hope Mirrlees Papers, Newnham College Archives, Cambridge, 6/5.

she would have called its 'pattern'. And from her present vantage-ground, it must seem not to matter particularly whether or not they are recorded – however, is one justified in acting upon <u>that</u> assumption? I mean, should one not be governed by what one knows the person thought when they were alive?[35]

Here Hope echoes Harrison's final words in her own memoir – in which Jane also refuses to discuss her life after Cambridge because her years in Paris were 'too present' and 'too intimate' – and so the prolonged effort to retell Jane's life came to an end.

There is little evidence to suggest that Hope ever completed another novel after *Lud-in-the-Mist*. One entry in a notebook of the 1940s hints at what may have stood in the way of her publishing.

> Showing MS to a priest
> I want to know 1) whether there is anything in it contrary to Catholic faith or morals 2) Whether there is anything scandalising. But I do not wish for the criterion for the latter to be the prudery of the lower-middle classes.

All her work to date could conceivably have been seen as blasphemous – she tackled the Catholic Church and faith in one way or another in at least two of her novels as well as in *Paris*. But it is unclear what manuscript is under the priest's scrutiny here. If it is a novel, then no record of it remains. During her dalliances with Jane's biography, Hope had begun another project in the 1930s, *A Fly in Amber: Being an Extravagant Biography of the Romantic Antiquary Sir Robert Bruce Cotton* – and this erratic, fascinating book would occupy her for the next thirty years. But it is impossible that this should be the manuscript she showed to her priest in the 1940s, for her biography would take decades yet to complete. One other possibility emerges from within the Mirrlees archive: an incomplete typescript of what appears to be an extended, possibly book-length, essay on the Christian mysteries of Incarnation, Communion, and the Passion, among others. Mirrlees states in her preface to the text: 'it is only by dint of a slow process of integration that the convert, from books, sermons and his own meditations, gains cognizance of these high matters. If this little book is able to hasten this process for some of its readers, it will not have been written in vain.' Her intention was to help recent

---

35 Hope Mirrlees to Jessie Stewart, 29 March 1943, Jane Harrison Collection, Newnham College Archives, Cambridge, 5/1/1.

converts to the Catholic Church understand some of its most complex ideas as well as to follow the simplest rituals of Mass. Mirrlees may have been anxious about potentially interpreting the Scriptures where it was not her place to do so, hence her wish to know if there was anything in her book 'contrary to Catholic faith or morals'. Whatever the reaction of her priest was, we do know that her book was never published. But her interest in making plain the ritual aspects of Catholic devotion is reminiscent of Harrison's work on Greek ritual, especially its cult practices. Mirrlees even alludes to Jane in draft notes for her book – in a somewhat sacrilegious way – when trying to explain how a convert might conjure sympathy for Christ's suffering:

> When I first became a Catholic, I was worried at not being moved by the thought of our Lord's sufferings, and I found that if I pictured Him with the face of a dear friend who had died not long before, I was instantly moved to an agony of tenderness. But I did not often do it because I felt a little doubtful as to whether or not it was permissible. Since then a priest whom I consulted on the difficult problem as to how much love of the creature interferes with the love of God, told me that one ought to make oneself realise, by meditation, that what one loves in the creature are found also in God. If one does this, inevitably, it seems to me, one comes to picture our Lord looking like the person one loves best – and in time, I believe and hope, one will come truly mystically to love the creature in Christ, to love Christ in the creature.[36]

In other words – if we take this face of a beloved friend to be Jane's – Hope's conversion after Harrison's death might have transferred the mourning process into something more lasting: faith. The love of Christ and the love of the creature or mortal (which, in Hope's notebooks, is sometimes tied up with desire or sin) find themselves problematically combined.

The death of Hope's mother in 1948 may have been a contributing factor in her decision to leave England that year; she took up residence in South Africa, at Molenvliet in Stellenbosch, thirty miles from Cape Town, and lived there until the early 1960s. Drawn perhaps by her family's connections, Hope's intention was to settle in South Africa permanently – she shipped all her books,

---

36 Hope Mirrlees Papers, Newnham College Archives, Cambridge, 6/3/14 (ca. 1936). Mirrlees states that she wrote this essay in response to an article in *The Spectator* written by Father D'Arcy seven years previously, on 4 May 1929.

her Pekinese dog and her furniture and bought a house where she could enjoy the 'Mediterranean climate'. She wrote to Mary MacCarthy in 1949 that she was leading an 'Aunt-Sister-ish' life full of 'Rummy parties' – no doubt Gin Rummy – while her 'family' consisted of two native African servants, her housekeeper and, for a few months, 'a country lady from Midlothian' named Honor Clerk.[37] In 1950, with Honor present, Hope hosted travelling Bloomsbury connections Alix and James Strachey. Although Hope enjoyed the leisure of being on the outskirts of town, she did not retire from intellectual life – she made friends with the local academic community, among them Leo and Nellie Marquard. Leo Marquard was the Editorial Manager of Oxford University Press in Cape Town and Hope described his wife as a highly intelligent Lecturer in English at Stellenbosch University. Hope provided Nellie with a letter of introduction to the Newnham scholar Enid Welsford and she received a personalised copy of Hope's privately printed poetry collection. Hope was also acquainted with Irma Stern, a major painter who had studied at the Weimar Academy in her youth and was linked with the German Expressionists, but who became a significant artistic presence during her life in South Africa. While it is unclear how well the two women knew each other, one can certainly sense the natural colour of the region's landscape in both Stern's paintings and Hope's poems about South Africa. Another important friend during these years was the British novelist Mary Renault. Renault, with her long-time partner Julie Mullard, had moved to South Africa in 1948. Renault was a frequent visitor to Hope's home and the two women corresponded after Hope's return to Oxford.

The 1950s appear to have been full of travel – and much of this inspired the poems written in the three slim poetry volumes that appeared from the early 1960s to 1976 (*Poems*, *Moods and Tensions* and an expanded, revised edition of the latter). Hope made frequent research trips to England for her Cotton biography in the 1950s, staying in London or with her sister Margot at Bicester House, her home near Oxford. *A Fly in Amber* was published by Faber and Faber in 1962, after being nurtured for many years by T.S. Eliot's constant support. Two oversized scrapbooks, filled with postcards and historical facts, offer a glimpse into her travels to Europe and America.[38] With Margot, Hope went on a 'heavenly'

---

37 Hope Mirrlees to Mary MacCarthy, 2 December 1949, Mary MacCarthy Papers, Courtesy, The Lilly Library, Indiana University, Bloomington, Indiana.

motoring holiday through Italy in 1959. They hired a Fiat in Milan and drove from Ravenna to Florence, Pisa and finally ended up in Rome. The two women mined their tour books for sights (often religious) and Hope carefully documented her impressions and made notes on her reading about Italian architecture. Earlier that year, Hope had driven through New England, arriving first in New York and then heading off though Connecticut, Massachusetts and Maine. She was given a guided tour of the Yale University Library and taken into the basement (to see the Boswells) by the head librarian. New York City's skyline stunned her as it had some of the early European modernists decades before: she called it a 'giant primeval forest' and a 'splendid nightmare', making a note of the best restaurants and the best bourbon.

Hope's life at The Firs, a large stone house set upon a hill, in Headington, near Oxford, is remembered by the few that visited her there. Among them were Valerie Eliot, the Oxford scholar and poet Mary Lascelles, members of her family and the occasional academic in search of information about her literary past. One of these scholars, Suzanne Henig, then Professor of English at San Diego State University, went as far as to attempt Hope's literary resurrection. Henig provided a long biographical introduction to a republished (and bowdlerised) version of *Paris*, which Hope had edited for potential blasphemy. Henig produced a recording of Hope reading *Paris* during her trip in the early 1970s and had hoped to write a biography of Hope, but these plans were quickly scuttled by Hope's own unwillingness to be the object of scrutiny. Their correspondence, of which only Henig's letters are available, is full of obvious infatuation.[39] But it is clear that her (oft repeated) belief in Hope's genius was not enough to secure the biography. It appears that Henig – who wrote an account of the Hogarth Press only to have it rejected by Woolf's executors – was writing Hope into a larger, often scandalous, history of Bloomsbury, one that Hope no longer wished to be a part of. In a 1972 letter, Henig writes 'By the way – yes, I think Jane H. loved you. How could she help it?' Hope was reluctant to publish a biographical account of her years with Jane; therefore one can imagine that, so many years later, the prospect of having her own life laid bare was not to her liking. But Henig's efforts are still among the first to bring

38 Hope Mirrlees Papers, Newnham College Archives, Cambridge, 6/1.
39 Mirrlees's letters to Henig and the audiotape of *Paris* are in a private collection and inaccessible. Quotations from Henig's letters are taken from Hope Mirrlees Papers, Newnham College Archives, Cambridge, 2/2/4.

Mirrlees's work back into view. In Hope's final years, *Lud-in-the-Mist* was rediscovered and republished (without Hope's knowledge). It was read aloud on BBC radio: the producers had assumed the author was dead. In 1976, the Amate Press brought out a more comprehensive edition of *Moods and Tensions*, in 350 numbered copies, with an introduction by Raymond Mortimer. He writes:

> Over fifty years ago Miss Hope Mirrlees bowled me over, first by the beauty of her bearing and cerulean eyes, a minute later by her dulcet voice and next by the charming acuteness of her talk: never previously had I met so seductive a bluestocking. [...] Happy the poet who is also a scholar, who can turn from her Euripides and Horace to memories of many talks with T.S. Eliot and Virginia Woolf, then stroll in her garden with her idolised pug. Her imagination is at home in Mytilene and the Sabine hills, in Venice, in Heian Japan and in Muscovy, no less than in the Siena of St Catherine and the Avila of St Teresa.

Mortimer's contrasting picture of Hope from her youth to the later life seems fitting; it accounts for her extensive learning and the vast imagination (spanning both pagan and orthodox theologies) that produced such drastically different works of literature. In one of her last notebooks, Hope jotted down a quotation from Virgil's *Eclogue 3* that comforted her when thinking of her own poetry and writing:

> Muses, my song begins in praise of Jove.
> He makes all flourish; my song is in his care.[40]

Nearer to her death and with her health failing – she had suffered bouts of pneumonia in 1975 – Hope spent her final weeks at the Thames Bank nursing home in Goring-on-Thames and died on 1 August 1978.

§

To return to an earlier question: what accounts for the difference between *Paris* and the poems from *Moods and Tensions* written forty years later? Of course, *Paris* is the product of a much younger poet and one cannot discredit the literary influences Hope would have

---

[40] The quotation from *Eclogue 3* in her notebook is slightly shorter: 'Iovis omnia plena; Ille colit terras, illi mea carmina curae.'

met with during her intermittent visits to and eventual residence in the city where her poem is set.

The significance to Mirrlees of the urban landscape of Paris is best borne out by her long psychogeographic poem *Paris*, printed in 1920 as the Hogarth Press's fifth publication, with a print run of only 175 copies. Recent scholarly interest in *Paris*, as a 'lost modernist masterpiece', has created a new generation of readers, appreciative of the poem's fragmentary and stream-of-consciousness aesthetic and its relevance to twentieth-century British and American poetry.[41] *Paris* was reprinted only once during Mirrlees's lifetime, in 1973 by the *Virginia Woolf Quarterly* (edited by Henig). In 1946, Hope had rejected a request from Leonard Woolf to reissue the poem. Virginia Woolf, on publishing *Paris*, remarked that it was 'obscure, indecent, and brilliant'.[42] Woolf understood the primacy of Mirrlees's experimental verse; indeed its only true predecessor – as Mirrlees herself acknowledged – was Jean Cocteau's *Le Cap de Bonne-Espérance*, published in 1919. The similarities between Mirrlees's poem and Cocteau's are significant, not the least of which is the mention of 'BYRRH' and 'St. John at Patmos'. It is possible that Mirrlees was present during Cocteau's reading of his poem at Adrienne Monnier's Paris bookshop; Cocteau had slyly arranged for André Gide to be present and Gide brought his young lover Marc Allegret – both were friends of Mirrlees and Harrison. She might also have been influenced by Gertrude Stein, whom she met prior to writing *Paris*. In 1914 she invited Stein to lunch at Newnham College to meet (a rather uninterested) Harrison, and Stein also stayed at the Mirrlees family home in Cambridge. Whilst in Paris studying Russian it does appear that Hope and Jane read the poetry of the Russian Futurist Vladimir Mayakovsky (*A Cloud in Trousers* perhaps?) and that Hope may have benefited from the energy and scope of Mayakovsky's work.

Paris is without a doubt a modernist poem and although we have fewer indications of definite avant-garde influences than we might like, we can at least guess at what types of (French) poets Mirrlees might have benefited from reading. As there is no hard evidence – there are no surviving complete manuscripts, drafts, or notes for *Paris* – we must rely on what little can be pieced together

---

41 Julia Briggs introduced a facsimile copy of *Paris* in the anthology of modernist women's writing *Gender in Modernism*, ed. Bonnie Kime Scott, pp. 261–303. Briggs's detailed notes for *Paris* are reprinted in this edition.

42 Virginia Woolf, letter to Margaret Llewelyn Davies, 17 August 1919, in *Letters*, Vol. II, p. 385.

from her letters.[43] Just prior to composing *Paris*, Mirrlees had finished work on her first novel, *Madeleine*. In part, *Madeleine* takes its subject from the life of the seventeenth-century literary hostess Madame de Scudéry (1607-1701) and her circle of *précieuses*. Mirrlees's interest in Mme de Scudéry, her salons (referred to as *samedi* after their designated day), and the happenings at the Hôtel de Rambouillet (the first literary salon in France, which Mme de Scudéry attended and wrote society novels about) would seem at odds with the 'modern' spirit of her poem. On her visit to Paris in 1913, Hope read at the Bibliothèque Nationale (she was researching for *Madeleine*); she also dined with her friend Karin Costelloe's mother and stepfather, the British art historian Bernard Berenson. The only other significant contact Mirrlees seems to have had was the ageing English poet and Pre-Raphaelite sympathiser Mary Robinson, or as she was better known in France, Madame Duclaux, at her residence on the fashionable rue de Rivoli. By the time Hope made the acquaintance of Duclaux and the poet Anna de Noailles, the two ageing *salonnières* were well past the height of their careers. (By 1913, Noailles' health was so delicate that she held court propped up on pillows from her Louis XV bed.) Duclaux – whose coterie included some of the most celebrated thinkers of 1880s London, including Pater, Symons, Morris, the Rossetti siblings, and Ford Madox Brown – was herself a proponent of *fin-de-siècle* aestheticism, intended to fill the gap left by a steady wane of Pre-Raphaelitism and accelerated by the death of Dante Gabriel Rossetti in 1882. Duclaux's poetry was widely admired by her contemporaries, especially the collections *The New Arcadia* (1884) and *An Italian Garden* (1886). 'The Ideal' (from *An Italian Garden*) is just one of Robinson's poems from the perspective of a *flâneuse* walking on a moonlit night in 'the streets where all the world may go.'

> For in my Soul a temple I have made,
>   Set on a height, divine and steep and far,
> Nor often may I hope those floors to tread,
>   Or reach the gates that glimmer like a star.

Here, the speaker's ideal destination is more metaphysical than real and the *flâneuse* inverts the wandering to a spiritual inner

---

43 Two proof pages – typescript with handwritten annotations by Mirrlees – have survived. One senses from the changes Mirrlees requested of Woolf (possibly quite close to printing), that she was very particular about both the content and typography and that the poem was still evolving even at this late stage.

world. The language of distances, of anxiety between public and private space, reappears throughout her work, as in the poem 'Venetian Nocturne'.

> Down the narrow Calle where the moonlight
>   cannot enter
>   The houses are so high;
> Silent and alone we pierced the night's dim
>   core and centre –
>   Only you and I.

The speaker's destination is never a physical place – the 'narrow dark' leads to death; wandering is toil, is life. In terms of Victorian femininity, the appropriate place for this kind of metaphorical walking is indoors or in the mind, or at that artificial boundary that is the literary salon, that psychical gateway between the street and the inner privacy of home. As Ana Parejo Vadillo points out in her essay on Robinson's 'at homes' in Bloomsbury and Kensington: 'London salons were, because of their hybrid nature, spaces that linked the private and public, home and street, and the woman poet with the passenger and the *flâneuse*.'[44] It is possible that Robinson, who appears to have been a friend to both Hope and Jane, introduced Hope in 1913 to Anna de Noailles, the Madame de Scudéry of her day. Robinson, who had emigrated to France and married a Frenchman, maintained close ties with French literati. Offering her opinion to her ex-countrymen in 1913, she wrote in *The Times* that Noailles was 'the greatest poet that the twentieth century has produced in France – perhaps in Europe'.[45] Noailles had the distinction afforded to many wealthy, aristocratic women of beauty, power and intellect: she was adored by the famous literary men who sought patronage, refuge or even simply the electricity of her presence. The Comtesse wrote several novels and produced over 1,900 pages of poetry; she received countless honours for her contributions to French literature and counted Proust, Cocteau, and Collette as her friends and admirers. In the years since her death, her poetry has been retrospectively seen as overly 'feminine', and indeed her work may appear (to those who

---

44 Ana Parejo Vadillo, 'Aestheticism "At Home" in London: A. Mary F. Robinson and the Aesthetic Sect', in *London Eyes: Reflections in Text and Image*, ed. Gail Cunningham and Stephen Barber (New York: Berghahn Books, 2007), pp. 59–78 (p. 64).

45 Quoted in Catherine Perry, *Persephone Unbound: Dionysian Aesthetics in the Works of Anna de Noailles* (Lewisburg: Bucknell University Press, 2003), p. 21.

gender effusive displays of emotion as 'female') too heightened, too dramatic, too much 'of the body'. And yet she was certainly a poet of the senses, and a nationalist. Importantly, Mirrlees read Noailles before the two women met in 1913, and Hope appears to have translated one of her poems, 'The Invocation', into English at some point after it was published in *Les Éblouissements* (Dazzling Lights) in 1907. Mirrlees's translation, which is in her archive, begins:

> Heart's city – listen while I sing to you – 'tis night,
>   I come with heavy arms that all the world's love hold
>   And poets, long since dead, down in their graves so cold
>   Pursue me with desires, and know that *I* now live.
>
> I am Time's sister; and the song that never dies;
>   That shrill and burning cry, that makes the deep woods ring
>   The adoration of the plants for Spring;
>   Man's god-like haughty longing for the skies.

The speaker and the lyric 'I' incorporate the many ancestral voices of the living and the dead in this 'city'. And, much like *Paris*'s 'I', Noailles' speaker tries to rid herself of the fractious multiplicities that threaten to overwhelm her:

> Go! I can house you no longer within my heart,
>   Spirits of hot regrets and dreams. Become again
>   The spirits of the fire, the woods, the rain
>   Depart from out my life – I bid you all depart.

On the whole, Hope's version of Noailles' poem is faithful to the original, bar one change that reinterprets the poem's overall meaning. Mirrlees translates the first words of Noailles' poem as 'Heart's city', when the French is simply 'Ma ville' or 'My city'. This change, which on the surface is so obviously different, could not have been made unwittingly. The city itself, if one wants to pin the Comtesse's poem to an actual locale, is undoubtedly Paris. And, perhaps not coincidentally, Noailles' first collection of poetry was *Le Coeur innombrable* (The Innumerable Heart), which Mirrlees would surely have known. For Noailles, the heart becomes the metaphoric seat of the individual 'I' *and* the plurality of Man, memory, even civilisation and nationhood. The penultimate stanza reads:

> And then, set free of this my heart's fierce burn,
>   Bearing no more the world attached to me,

> At last, I may repose beneath a great, calm tree,
> And with some pure fresh water fill my urn.

The seeking of higher ground that occurs at the end of Mirrlees's *Paris* and the refusal to be overwhelmed by the rising waters of dreams, the dead and the city's inhabitants is similar to these lines from Noailles' poem. The key to *Paris* is this very corporeal multiplicity of one: 'Paris is a huge home-sick peasant, / He carries a thousand villages in his heart.' This ability to fracture the speaker's consciousness (only to restore its wholeness later) was perhaps suggested by the act of translating Noailles' poem.

The greatest difficulty in finding an alternative lineage of influence for *Paris*, one that does not merely assume that Mirrlees imbibed avant-garde poetic principles (Cubist or otherwise) and set about constructing a poem, is that the evidence of her actual milieu points to authors whose work is highly formal, even archaic. If Mirrlees's taste in painting – she felt the true test of a picture's worth was whether or not it would be at home in the Louvre – is anything to go by, it is likely that she was more individually minded than those who imagine her seated studying a copy of *Nord-Sud* might allow. Mirrlees never wrote anything like *Paris* again, and if it was an experiment with form, brought on by the artistic and political climate of 1919 Paris, then the poem's genius is all the more extraordinary for it. It is possible that *Paris* benefits from Duclaux and Noailles' figure of the *flâneuse*, and it is likely that the social, modern mode of femininity that increasingly became an acceptable urban presence was mediated and learnt in part from the model of the literary salon (Mirrlees was, by all accounts, an enchanting conversationalist). Mirrlees understood the importance of the public figure of the artist/poet/*flâneuse*, and in this sense *Paris* can be justifiably seen as the bridge between French models and T.S. Eliot's *The Waste Land*, which was begun in 1921. Briggs has theorised that Eliot may have read *Paris* before writing his poem, and as a Hogarth author (his formal collection *Poems* immediately preceded *Paris*'s publication) he would surely have known of its existence. Given the chance many years later, in an interview, to align her experiment with Eliot's famous poem, Mirrlees would not be drawn on conjectural similarities and simply said she did not know if he had read it, though the two were for many years intimate friends.

Paris is a daylong (though virtually impossible in 'real-time') psychogeographical *flânerie* through the streets and metro tunnels of post-World War I Paris. The poet records her surroundings in instances that are as ephemeral as her subjects; historical monuments share equal ground with advertisements for tobacco and coffee. The poem begins:

> I want a holophrase
>
> NORD-SUD
>
> ZIG-ZAG
> LION NOIR
> CACAO BLOOKER
>
> Black-figured vases in Etruscan tombs
> RUE DU BAC (DUBONNET)
> SOLFERINO (DUBONNET)
> CHAMBRES DES DEPUTES
>
> Brekekekek coax coax we are passing under the Seine
>
> DUBONNET
>
> The Scarlet Woman shouting BYRRH and deafening St. John at Patmos
>
> *Vous descendez Madame?*
>
> [...]
> CONCORDE
>
> I can't
> I must go slowly

The sounds and signs of the newly-opened Paris metro lead the reader above ground on a journey through the gardens, museums, and history of the city. The other side of *Paris*'s story, the poem's inception, its inspiration as well as the symbolic function of the city, comes to us in fragments of correspondence, diaries and, indeed, silences. In Mirrlees's archived correspondence very few mentions of *Paris* exist; besides those from Leonard and Virginia Woolf, the poem's publishers, two other letters from literary friends make an oblique reference to its existence: one from the French poet Jean Tardieu, and another from the proto-fascist writer Pierre Drieu La Rochelle. Drieu La Rochelle's letter simply states 'Your poem both moved and amused me greatly.'[46] Tardieu bemoans his inability to read *Paris* in English, but his admiration for Mirrlees's abilities is nonetheless unshaken: 'I am strongly drawn to and intrigued by

'Paris'. [...] But you, how I envy you, for you need never face the danger of being boring. In conversation you convey such gems of ideas, ingenious, gay and comical. Your very lyricism is, it is easy to deduce, of a precious quality. And yet you modestly disguise it with your humour.'[47] Gauging from the overall tenor of these letters, both men were clearly charmed by her, and there is a pseudo-romantic tone that irks. Nowhere is the sense that her poem made a real impression on her fellow writers, that it was recognised for employing largely French experiments in language and typography in an English-language poem. On the whole, the reviews *Paris* received in the British press were negative. The most damning appeared in *The Times Literary Supplement*.

> This little effusion looks at the first blush like an experiment in Dadaism; but there is method in the madness which peppers the pages with spluttering and incoherent statement displayed with various tricks of type. It seems meant by a sort of futurist trick to give an ensemble of the sensations offered to a pilgrim through Paris. But it is certainly not a 'Poem,' though we follow the author's guidance in classing it as such. To print the words 'there is no lily of the valley' in a vertical column of single letters might be part of a nursery game. It does not belong to the art of poetry.[48]

While it's no great surprise that the reviewer is resistant to 'tricks of type', or worse to that European anti-art bogey Dadaism, one senses that the gulf between *Paris* and the reviewer's taste is couched in a formalist sense of (British) poetic tradition; even the curious terms employed here, which are so much of the body, especially the female body – 'blush', 'spluttering', 'effusion', 'sensation' – mean to diffuse any potential danger ('trick') to the established 'art of poetry'.

In a 1925 letter to the artist Gwen Raverat, a mutual friend of Hope and Virginia, Woolf called the city of Paris a 'hostile brilliant alien city' – but in what way was Paris hostile?[49] Certainly we can imagine that how Woolf felt Paris was disconcertingly unfamiliar,

---

46 Letter from Pierre Drieu La Rochelle to Hope Mirrlees, 27 September 1921, Hope Mirrlees Papers, Newnham College Archives, Cambridge. Translated by Sura Qadiri.
47 Letter from Jean Tardieu to Hope Mirrlees, 17 October 1923, Hope Mirrlees Papers, Newnham College Archives, Cambridge. Translated by Sura Qadiri.
48 'Paris A Poem by Hope Mirrlees', *The Times Literary Supplement*, 6 May 1920.
49 Letter to Gwen Raverat, 8 April 1925, in *Letters*, Vol. III, p. 177.

she also recognised the 'brilliance' of Mirrlees's poem through its obscure, alien typography. Typesetting *Paris* proved incredibly frustrating for Woolf, who made several errors, some of which made it into the final Hogarth edition. Two proof pages survive with Mirrlees's handwritten amendments – and it is intriguing that she was still rewriting the poem at this late stage.[50] Whether or not Woolf liked the city (or for that matter, Mirrlees's poem), she occasionally made mention of her personal discomfort in Paris – possibly an all too English bias or a patronising evaluation of Parisian 'artistes'. There is evidence of both. In a letter to Hope, written in 1923, Woolf airs plans to visit her and Jane at the American Women's Club. She and Leonard would, en route to the Raverats in Vence, spend a night in Paris in their own 'speechless British way'.[51] But Woolf also observes elsewhere that 'myriads of the ineffective English' like Hope and Nancy Cunard (another Hogarth Press poet with difficult typography) flit from 'rock to rock' in Paris, hinting at the frivolity of life in the throes of European bohemia and outside the expectations of British society.[52] Although there is no evidence that Cunard and Mirrlees knew each other personally, it would appear that both women felt similarly about the freedoms life outside England might provide for them, for which Woolf had little sympathy.

After a dedication to the city of Paris, the poem begins with 'I': 'I want a holophrase'. A holophrase, a term Harrison used in her work *Themis* (1912), is defined as a primitive linguistic structure that expresses a complex concept in a single word or short phrase. Harrison describes holophrases as 'utterances of a relation in which the subject and object have not yet got their heads above water but are submerged in a situation.'[53] The holophrase predates 'Parts of Speech', which are a means of negotiating boundaries between the outside world and the inner consciousness of perception. As language is indeterminate in the holophrase, so is the positionality of the speaker. Of course 'want' is a kind of holophrase – and it also puns on want, as in 'to lack'. The poem begins with the utterance of the self, but it is a self on the verge of primitive language, precipiced on its own desire, and inundated

50 Details of these revisions can be found in the Commentary on *Paris*, pp. 121–2 (lines 290–3).
51 Woolf, letter to Hope Mirrlees, 6 January 1923, Hope Mirrlees Papers, Series III, Box I, Special Collections, University of Maryland Libraries.
52 Woolf, letter to Gwen Raverat, 8 April 1925, in *Letters*, Vol. III, p. 177.
53 Jane Ellen Harrison, *Themis* (Cambridge: Cambridge University Press, 1912), pp. 473–5.

with communicative and non-communicative language. Its opening is also an invocation, and, as the poem continues, it points back to the traditions of classical epic. Phrases like '*Vous descendez madame?*', a common expression on the metro trains, and the language-litter of advertisements and street signs mix with these few oracular 'I's. Further down the first page, an image of sin and of Christian prophesy combine: 'The Scarlet Woman shouting BYRRH [a French drink made by mixing red wine and tonic water] and deafening St. John at Patmos.' The 'I' ascends at the Place de la Concorde, itself a historical site of both reconciliation and public execution, and confronted by this underlying sense of danger, exclaims 'I can't / I must go slowly'. One imagines that the speaker's resistance, 'I can't', and her determination 'I must', is hesitation at the self's uniformity being threatened; it reminds us of Pound's famous ascension at the Place de la Concorde and the apparition of the uniform and deathly crowd in his 1913 poem 'A Station of the Metro'. Mirrlees's poet-*flâneur* encounters ghosts and spirits, fallen soldiers and peasants – and these are the real sights of Paris, not the Étoile, the Bois de Boulogne, or the Arc de Triomphe, which are variously boring and loathed by the speaker. The 'I' is wading 'knee deep in dreams' and later these dreams 'have reached' her waist – reminiscent of the submerging of subject and object by holophrases – and threaten to drown her.

> The ghost of Père Lachaise
> Is walking the streets,
> He is draped in a black curtain embroidered with the
> letter H,
>
> He is hung with paper wreaths,
> He is beautiful and horrible and the close friend of
> Rousseau, the official of the Douane.
>
> The unities are smashed,
> The stage is thick with corpses. . . .

'H' for 'Hope' but also for 'histoire': Paris balances death, literary immortals at Père Lachaise cemetery, and the unnamed speaker's initial as the poem's dead or soon-to-be-dead author; the poem is an attempt at immortality.[54] Another section of the poem encapsulates the city's power:

---

54 Briggs offers an alternative reading based on the historical figure of Père Lachaise, a seventeenth-century cleric. See Commentary on *Paris*, p. 118 (lines 175–7).

> What time
> Subaqueous
> Cell on cell
> Experience
> Very slowly
> Is forming up
> Into something beautiful – awful – huge
>   The coming to . . . . . .
> Thick halting speech – the curse of vastness.

'I can't', 'I want' and 'I must' – the language of resistance, sin and confession – is the 'thick halting speech', the breaking down of identity and individual experience in favour of the life of the city that threatens to destroy the 'I'. Eventually, Mirrlees finds higher ground towards the end of her poem, and is safe in her hotel on the rue de Beaune. She gazes down in a trance from the top floor and welcomes the new day just about to dawn. The poem ends with the symbol of the constellation Ursa Major, the bear – as do all of Hope's works before 1926 – pointing always to the north, to that pinnacle of hope.[55] She finds solace and comfort in the sign of the bear, her departure from the poem and a kind of acknowledged signature shared by her and Jane Harrison. It would be wrong to characterise the 'hostility' of Paris to the 'I' as negative. Indeed, the liberation from personality and personal history is no tragedy here – one returns to it, is safe, is able to be witness to everything without ever really being in danger. The Paris of tourists is 'two-dimensional', unreal and uninteresting. Paris's real appeal is not just the anonymity it provides, an argument one could make for any number of expatriates (lesbian or otherwise) who found community there in the early twentieth century. More importantly, Paris liberates the speaker from individual life and experience: the unutterable phrase is heaped with more complex language, which communicates nothing. And so is the self. The self returns to its private, secret tongue.

§

In this edition, the poems from the section 'Moods and Tensions' were originally published in three volumes, two of which were

---

[55] It is also worth noting that all three sections of Dante Alighieri's *Divine Comedy* end with the word 'stars'. The significance of stars as the end of a symbolic cycle of rebirth, restoration or return may have informed Mirrlees's choice.

privately printed (possibly in the mid-1960s). The final, lengthier edition (Mirrlees added four poems) appeared in 1976 from the Amate Press.[56] Robin Waterfield, with the antiquarian bookseller David Low, founded the Amate Press in 1973 after returning from Iran, where he had worked as a Christian missionary and run children's homes. Mirrlees was introduced to Waterfield by Margaret Ellis (later one of Hope's literary executors), who would assist her in compiling a second (still unpublished) volume to *A Fly in Amber: Being an Extravagant Biography of the Romantic Antiquary Sir Robert Bruce Cotton*.[57] Hope completed *Moods and Tensions* in 1975, making a last-minute addition to the collection: 'Jesus Wept', a short poem about unmourned death, which Ellis took down as Hope recited it. But the poems in these volumes are by no means dashed off at the moment of inspiration. Hope's notebooks – many of which are devoted to obsessive and careful rewritings of a single poem or parts of a poem – are the product of years of research and thought. And some of the poems she planned either never came to any acceptable form or she chose not to include them in *Moods and Tensions*.

The most significant of these is a poem based on Keats and his 'love of fruit'. Drafts of the poem borrow heavily from Keats's letters to Fanny Brawne and ruminate on death (and its counterpart, youth) while intermittently returning to the idea that 'Fruit is a fairy sacrament'. Her plans were to call it 'Three Variations on the theme of Keats's Death', to be written in three parts – the first two of which would be entitled 'A Meditation on Keats's Love of Fruit' and 'The Ceiling (Tasso and the Jesuit Saint)'. At one stage, she wished to write all three sections in different metres. The lure of fruit as carnal sin repeats like a mantra, as does the delight in transgression, in the tasting. The following quotation found in Hope's notebooks is taken from Keats's letter to his sister in 1819:

> Give me Books, fruit, French wine, and fine weather and a little music out of doors [. . .] I should like now to promenade round your Gardens – apple-tasting – pear-tasting – plum-judging – apricot-nibbling – peach-scrunching – nectarine-sucking and melon-carving: I have a great feeling for antiquated cherries full of sugar cracks – and a white currant tree kept for company. I admire lolling on a lawn by a water lilied pond to eat white

---

56 See Note on the Text for specific details about these three editions.
57 This volume is in completed typescript and is entitled *The Lost Pearl*, Hope Mirrlees Papers, Newnham College Archives, Cambridge, 7/2/1.

currants and see gold-fish: and go to the Fair in the Evening if I'm good.[58]

To say this is the opposite of Hope's apparent Catholic asceticism would be to miss the point. Surely sin without a foreknowledge of sin fails to tantalise. And Keats's description of 'soft, pulpy, slushy, oozy' fruit melting down his throat is an imagined indulgence in sin exteriorised for the pleasure of others. Hope reads these letters as an admission to sin – and exhorts the figure of the dead poet to repent, intoning in verse: 'Pray! Pray!'. For Hope, fruit stands in for his passion for Fanny Brawne. She notes:

> Summary
> Fanny is death and fruit and the Belle Dame, and the True Thomas's Queen who gives the apple of vision. She is <u>forbidden</u> fruit – the basket of strawberries he never got at school. He had suffered (when jealous) the torments of Catullus – but without cause. Passion fruit 'Ripeness is all'. Lear was old, but not ripe. Perhaps Keats was ripe and just about to rot.

The poem was never finished, possibly because she could not exert the same control over the material that one senses from the formal poems of *Moods and Tensions*. For Mirrlees, rhyme is one of the primary devices that dictates the flow and meaning of her message – often whilst balancing issues like sin and death.

The poems from *Moods and Tensions* are full of literary, classical and theological references – they are the multilayered impressions of the present moment imbued with personal and historical significance, so much so that the poems' 'I' is often detached and unidentifiable behind the heavily syllabic ring of the metre. 'The Copper-Beech at St. Giles' Churchyard' recounts a walk through that site, surrounded by the golden colour of the tree: 'And wrapped in gold I thought about my past, / And all the dreams that life has blown away'. These are the poem's most personal lines – elsewhere Mirrlees deflects questions of her own mortality through the natural world, which answers: 'do not fear, / Love, only love, can be the answer *here*. / Take heart of grace, in your beginning is your end.' The divine refrain, with its ring of Eliot's own lines, is spoken from the mouths of doves.

'Et in Arcadia Ego' begins: 'I have no wish to eat forbidden fruit,

---

58 John Keats letter to Fanny Keats, 28 August 1819, in *Letters of John Keats to his family and friends*, ed. Sidney Colvin (London: Macmillan, 1891), p. 285.

/ I did not gather roses when I might, / Now I am old and cold, / The years begin to turn on me and bite.' The speaker is haunted by the 'uninvited spectre' of Charles Baudelaire, whose grave, in the cemetery of Montparnasse, Hope used to tend with Jane Harrison. The anxieties of life's failure pile up: 'Your only crops are dreams, your only sheaves'. Two poems, 'The Legend of the Painted Room' and 'A Portrait of the Second Eve, Painted in Pompeian Red', are based on scenes from two different rooms with painted walls: the first is the site of a medieval tavern in Oxford where Shakespeare was said to have drank, and the second is in the 'Bacchic' Villa dei Misteri in Pompeii. Both fascinate the poet for the same reason – their secret, ritual histories of revelry. Her poem, 'A Meditation on Donatello's Annunciation in the Church of Santa Croce, Florence', and the 'Second Eve' are among the best in *Moods and Tensions*. Here the poet's presence is minimal and the tense reticence of the speaker does not distract from the poem's wider, aesthetic and religious argument.

The poems from *Moods and Tensions* will not necessarily appeal to those who admire *Paris*. Their tone is sometimes archaic and a poem like 'A Doggerel Epitaph for My Little Dog Sally' is written solely to amuse (and to commemorate the loss of a much-loved pet). But these highly idiosyncratic and polished poems record the progress of a poet through the arduous task of scholarship – in letters to Jessie Stewart, Hope continually prioritised her ongoing work on Cotton's biography over the writing of Harrison's life. Hope wrote in an undated notebook that all of her books 'finish by taking the shape of E.W.'s [Elder Wife's] philosophy'. The consistent praise of Mirrlees's friends and readers – Mary Renault, John Betjeman, A.L. Rowse, Peter Levi, and Mary Lascelles among others – was that her poetry was 'learned'. Indeed, this is the typical defence against poetry that precludes the self. But traces of Harrison's influence remain – especially in the Bacchic/Orphic rituals of 'Second Eve' – and the memories of the poet's life as a young woman in Paris and Cambridge are evident here. Her model is still the classical world and even her asceticism points back to Harrison's quotation of a letter from Keats to his sister-in-law at the close of her last critical work *Epilegomena* (1921):

> Notwithstanding your happiness and your recommendation I hope I shall never marry. Though the most beautiful Creature were waiting for me at the end of a Journey or a Walk; though the Carpet were of Silk; the Curtains of the morning Clouds; the

> chairs and Sofa stuffed with Cygnet's down, the food Manna, the Wine beyond Claret, the Window opening on Winander mere, I should not feel – or rather my Happiness would not be so fine, as my Solitude is sublime. Then, instead of what I have described, there is a sublimity to welcome me home – The roaring of the wind is my wife and the Stars through the window-pane are my Children. [. . .] I feel more and more every day, as my imagination strengthens, that I do not live in this world alone, but in a thousand worlds – No sooner am I alone than shapes of epic greatness are stationed around me and serve my Spirit the office which is equivalent to a King's bodyguard [. . .][59]

Epilegomena can be read as the scholar looking back over decades of work and re-evaluating her theories in a modern age of religious doubt. Harrison asks, what is the function of religion in the contemporary world and how has it evolved since Antiquity? Religion, she contends, should not merely condemn what is 'evil', it should be means to a betterment of life and that path requires a degree of asceticism. Not asceticism in terms of the denial of desire, but more of the Ancient Greek idea – a way to strengthen and refine the self. During the time that Hope was writing her novel *Lud-in-the-Mist* she expressed a similar idea about sublimity.

> In my two published novels and in the one I am at present writing I have found myself automatically in spite of myself fitting my observations into this ancient frame. Behind the interplay of the human passions is the old ritual fight between summer and winter; my heroes in spite of their modern dress, are jacks in the green dressed up in flowers and ribbons. I have sometimes thought that a fine novel might be written with a Christian background, grace and Sin, the invisible protagonists. Grace, slowly, ruthlessly moulding the circumstances of the hero. But that novel is not for me to write; for though grace and sin seem to me magnificent conceptions they are for me without reality. Absolute truth has little to do with fiction, but sincerity has a great deal. Another thing – once one's mind is pregnant, the faeries come. It is as if one were turned into an automatic bird-flower smeared with birdlime one stands motionless in a field, gazing at the clouds, preoccupied with one's own thoughts

---

[59] The original quotation from Keats' letter to Georgiana Keats, 25 October 1818, can be found in Colvin's *Letters*, p. 180. Harrison's version in *Epilegomena* has slightly different wording.

while all the time without the slightest effort on one's part the birds come and get entangled in the lime.[60]

Decades after she wrote the lines quoted above, it is all the more difficult to reconcile her preoccupation with Christian grace and sin with the playful pagan strain in her poetry. The balance is an uneasy one. An asymmetry between conceptions of love in a pre and post Christian world can be found in 'Crossed in Love' – a poem that seems to advocate self-sacrifice over the fulfilment of desire: 'The code of courtly love is that of Christ: / To take rebuffs and not resent the shame; / to bide with cheerfulness the broken tryst'. Some of the unpublished work is less guarded than those poems printed in *Moods and Tensions*. The 'old ritual fight', here and in Mirrlees's later poems, is re-enacted in both the natural (and necessarily pagan) world as well as in a Christian moral paradigm. And while the sin is never uttered – leaving us to our speculations – we should be comforted by the poet's own resistance to grace. Her method of escape: an imagination that is, to use Jane Harrison's word, vertumnal, hesitant, even a bit mischievous. The critic A.L. Rowse sent Hope a letter of praise in December 1966:

> It was most kind of you to send me your enchanting poems. I greatly enjoyed reading them – how gifted you are: they are not only charming and move one, but utterly natural and authentic, and entirely true to you – as poetry should be. And as so little is nowadays – pretentiously intellectual, by people who, intellectually speaking, are thoroughly second-rate. Why should *they* aspire to be so intellectual? They should leave it to people who have intellects.

Certainly Mirrlees's poetry is out of step with the experimentation of the 1960s; she had come a long way from being, technically at least, close to the 'pretentious' avant garde. It must be said that Hope's later poetry is, in a different way to that of *Paris*, very intellectual. But neither work should be taken as a more or less genuine representation of the poet's imagination.

---

60 Hope Mirrlees Papers, Newnham College Archives, Cambridge, 6/5/7. Compare these thoughts on the 'ancient frame' to Mirrlees's epigraph to *Lud-in-the-Mist*, taken from Harrison's *Prolegomena* (1921): 'The Sirens stand, as it would seem, to the ancient and the modern, for the impulses in life as yet immoralised, imperious longings, ecstasies, whether of love or art, or philosophy, magical voices calling to a man from his "Land of Heart's Desire," and to which if he hearken it may be that he will return no more – voices, too, which, whether a man sail by or stay to hearken, still sing on.'

As Mirrlees's contemporary, the modernist poet Mina Loy, wrote of Picasso: 'Out of millions of people there is always enough intellect to keep a masterpiece afloat – on the ocean of recognition – for a considerable length of time.'[61] It is my hope that this edition will encourage further study into Mirrlees's work and that her contribution to her generation can resurface.

---

61 Mina Loy Papers, Yale Collection of American Literature (MSS6), Beinecke Rare Book and Manuscript Library, Box 7, folder, 188, undated page. This note appears to be part of plans for an unpublished essay entitled 'The Misunderstand of Picasso'.

A Note on the Text

The Hope Mirrlees Papers were donated to the Newnham College Archives in March 2009 for the purpose of compiling this volume. Many of the previously unpublished poems in this edition have been taken from Hope's handwritten notebooks and, in all cases, the most final of these versions has been reprinted. Where relevant, further details about the nature of the poems' composition and placement within the notebooks are given in notes at the end of this edition. Mirrlees never assigned her name to poems in manuscript, but most of the poems included here are in her hand or are typescripts containing her handwritten corrections. It has been more difficult to verify provenance of typescript poems, therefore only those that are most likely to be written by Mirrlees have been included, a judgement premised on a sense of her poetic voice as well as biographical detail. It is worth noting that among Mirrlees's papers are unsigned typescripts of four published poems by her friend Mary Lascelles, which should not be confused as Mirrlees's own work. Lascelles, a Jane Austen scholar at Somerville College, Oxford, and an interesting poet in her own right, is the dedicatee of *Moods and Tensions*. Some minor edits have been made in the previously unpublished work – underlined phrases or words have been italicised, hyphens inserted where required and em and en dashes have been regularised.

Paris has been lightly edited to correct some of the spelling errors of the original Hogarth Press edition. The poem's complex layout utilises several idiosyncratic typographical effects, and these have been preserved as best as possible. In a recently published version in *Gender in Modernism* (2007), the poem appears to be divided into numbered sections, but this is a result of the preserved page numbers from the Hogarth layout. *Paris* should be read as a long and continuous poem, and therefore the Hogarth page numbers have been omitted here. The present volume also incorporates notes on the poem (which originally appeared in *Gender in Modernism*) by the scholar Julia Briggs, whose work on Mirrlees was among the first to restore *Paris* to the attention of scholars of modernism and the general reader. Details of Mirrlees's omissions and alterations to *Paris* for reprinting in the *Virginia Woolf Quarterly* have been appended to Briggs's original Commentary on *Paris*.

The poems in the 'Moods and Tensions' section of this edition are from three volumes published between the early 1960s and 1976, in a final dated edition by the Amate Press. The first volume, *Poems*, contains eight poems: 'Sickness and Recovery at the Cape of Good Hope in Spring'; 'Mothers'; 'The Death of Cats and Roses'; 'Bertha frightens Miss Bates'; 'Heaven is not Fairyland'; 'Gulls'; '"Une Maison commode, propre, et belle. . ."' and 'A Doggerel Epitaph for my Little Dog, Sally'. All of these poems reappeared in *Moods and Tensions* (in a different order), a privately printed edition of seventeen poems. Mirrlees heads an earlier draft of *Moods and Tensions*' table of contents 'Moods and Tenses'. The shift from 'tenses', which like 'mood' is a linguistic quality applied to verbs, to 'tensions' could be seen as a move from the concerns of language towards the poems' emotional content. While language and narrative are of course interwoven in Mirrlees's poems, 'tensions' raises the stakes and the reader is directed towards the 'mood' of the poet rather than the modality of the language. It is also worth noting that Jane Harrison's influence could be present in Mirrlees's original title; Harrison was a linguist and wrote at least two lectures on the Russian language, including one in 1919 (the year of *Paris*'s composition) about the evocative tenses of Russian verbs. Harrison was particularly taken with the 'imperfective' tense, which for her had an emotional impact similar to that of *durée* and ritual, because of its continual, repeated action. Mirrlees learned the Greek language from Harrison and followed her to the study of Russian during their extended visits to Paris in the 1910s and 1920s. Tellingly, Harrison writes in 1919 about certain aspects of Greek grammar that are comforting 'in the welter of tenses and moods that await one in the early stages of composition'.[62] Perhaps these poems of Mirrlees's, these 'moods and tenses', subconsciously or knowingly point back to Harrison's evocation of the writer's anxiety – only in Mirrlees's case not at the early stage of linguistic discovery, but near the end of her writing life, when perhaps the subtleties of tenses – past, present, future – were most intense.

Amate Press's *Moods and Tensions* contains twenty-one poems, those from the previous volumes and four new poems: 'The Legend of the Painted Room'; 'A Portrait of the Second Eve,

---

[62] Jane Ellen Harrison, *Aspects, Aorists and the Classical Tripos* (Cambridge: Cambridge University Press, 1919), p. 12.

Painted in Pompeian Red'; 'A Meditation on Donatello's Annunciation in the Church of Santa Croce, Florence' and 'Jesus Wept'. Hope's own proof copies of both *Moods and Tensions* are in her archive. Among her handwritten corrections (to the 1976 edition) in red ink are inserted hyphens, commas and slightly alternative wording. The most important changes are recorded in the Notes on the Poems. The *Virginia Woolf Quarterly* also published five of Mirrlees's poems in its inaugural issue (Fall 1972, pp. 24–7): 'Mothers'; 'The Glass Tánagra'; 'A Skull'; 'The Legend of the Painted Room' and 'A Doggerel Epitaph for my Little Bitch, Sally'. The only other literary journal that appears to have published poems from *Moods and Tensions* is the American magazine *POEM*, which printed five poems in March 1973 as part of a special feature on Mirrlees: 'Gulls'; 'Amor Fati'; Winter Trees'; 'The Land of Uz'; 'The Copper-Beech in St. Giles' Churchyard'.

This edition also includes six articles, all written and published by Mirrlees in the 1920s. The essay, 'Quelques aspects de l'art d'Alexis Mikhailovich Remizov', was originally published in translation in the French *Le Journal de Psychologie Normale et Pathelogique* in 1926. The version included here is taken from Mirrlees's English corrected typescript.

Select Bibliography

Works by Hope Mirrlees

Madeleine: One of Love's Jansenists (London: W. Collins, 1919)
Paris: A Poem (Richmond, London: Hogarth Press, 1919 [1920])
The Counterplot (London: W. Collins, 1924)
Life of the Archpriest Avvakum by Himself, translated with Jane Harrison (London: Hogarth Press, 1924)
The Book of the Bear, translated with Jane Harrison (London: Nonesuch Press, 1926)
Lud-in-the-Mist (London: W. Collins, 1926)
Poems, unknown publisher, ca. late 1950s/early 1960s
A Fly in Amber: being an extravagant biography of the romantic antiquary Sir Robert Bruce Cotton (London: Faber, 1962)
Moods and Tensions, unknown publisher, 1962
Paris (revised), *Virginia Woolf Quarterly* I.2 (1973), 4–17
Moods and Tensions: Seventeen Poems (Oxford: Amate Press, 1976)

Biographies and Sources

Robert Ackerman, *The Myth and Ritual School: JG Frazer and the Cambridge Ritualists* (London: Routledge, 2002)
Mary Beard, *The Invention of Jane Harrison* (Cambridge: Harvard University Press, 2000)
Julia Briggs, 'Hope Mirrlees and Continental Modernism', in *Gender in Modernism: New Geographies, Complex Intersections*, ed. Bonnie Kime Scott (Chicago: University of Illinois Press, 2007)
——, '"Printing Hope": Virginia Woolf, Hope Mirrlees, and the Iconic Imagery of *Paris*', in *Woolf in the Real World: Selected Papers from the Thirteenth International Conference on Virginia Woolf*, ed. Karen V. Kukil (Clemson, SC: Clemson University Digital Press, 2005)
Dora Carrington, *Dora Carrington: Letters and Extracts from her Diaries*, ed. David Garnett (London: Jonathan Cape, 1970)
Jean Cocteau, *Oeuvres poétiques completes*, ed. Michel Decaudin (Paris: Gallimard, 1999)
Lyndall Gordon, *T.S. Eliot: An Imperfect Life* (London: Vintage, 1998)
Jane Harrison, *Reminiscences of a Student's Life* (London: Hogarth Press, 1925)

——, *Themis: A Study of the Social Origins of Greek Religion* (1912) (London: Merlin Press, 1989)
Elisabeth Hausser, *Paris au jour le jour: les évenéments vus par la Presse, 1900–1919* (Paris: Les Editions de Minuit, 1968)
Suzanne Henig, 'Queen of Lud: Hope Mirrlees', *Virginia Woolf Quarterly* I.I (1972), 8–21
Patrice Higonnet, *Paris, Capital of the World*, trans. Arthur Goldhammer (Cambridge: Harvard University Press, 2002)
R. Brimley Johnson, *Some Contemporary Novelists (Women)* (London: Leonard Parsons, 1920)
Mary Lascelles, *The Adversaries and Other Poems* (Cambridge: Rampant Lions Press, 1971)
——, *Selected Poems*, privately printed, 1990
Margaret MacMillan, *Paris 1919: Six Months that Changed the World* (New York: Random House, 2002)
Katherine Mansfield, *The Collected Letters of Katherine Mansfield*, ed. Vincent O'Sullivan and Margaret Scott, Vol. 3, 1919–1920 (Oxford: Clarendon Press, 1993)
Emily Lina Mirrlees and Margaret Rosalys Coker, *Wishful Cooking* (London: Faber and Faber, 1949)
Sandra J. Peacock, *Jane Ellen Harrison: The Mask and the Self* (New Haven: Yale University Press, 1988)
Catherine Perry, *Persephone Unbound: Dionysian Aesthetics in the Works of Anne de Noailles* (Lewisburg, PA: Bucknell University Press, 2003)
Annabel Robinson, *The Life and Work of Jane Ellen Harrison* (Oxford: Oxford University Press, 2002)
John Saunders, 'Re-introduced: Hope Mirrlees's *Paris*', *The Wolf* 16 (November 2007), 8–10
Roger Shattuck, *The Banquet Years: The Origins of the Avant-Garde in France, 1885 to World War I* (London: Jonathan Cape, 1969)
Jessie G. Stewart, *Jane Ellen Harrison: A Portrait from Letters* (London: Merlin Press, 1959)
Michael Swanwick, *Hope-in-the-Mist: The Extraordinary Career and Mysterious Life of Hope Mirrlees* (New Jersey: Temporary Culture, 2009)
Alice B. Toklas, *What is Remembered* (New York: Holt, Rinehart and Winston, 1963)
Ruth Vanita, *Sappho and the Virgin Mary: Same-Sex Love and the English Literary Imagination* (New York: Columbia University Press, 1996), 136–64
Virginia Woolf, *The Diary of Virginia Woolf*, ed. Anne Olivier Bell, Vols 1–5 (London: Hogarth Press, 1977–84)
——, *The Letters of Virginia Woolf*, ed. Nigel Nicholson, Vols 1–6 (London: Hogarth Press, 1975–1980)
Howard J. Woolmer, *A Checklist of the Hogarth Press, 1917–1938* (London: Hogarth Press, 1976)

Hope Mirrlees, ca. 1920

PARIS

A POEM

A
NOTRE DAME DE PARIS
EN RECONNAISSANCE
DES GRACES ACCORDEES

I want a holophrase

NORD-SUD

ZIG-ZAG
LION NOIR
CACAO BLOOKER

Black-figured vases in Etruscan tombs

RUE DU BAC (DUBONNET)
SOLFERINO (DUBONNET)
CHAMBRE DES DEPUTES

Brekekekek coax coax we are passing under the Seine   10

DUBONNET

The Scarlet Woman shouting BYRRH and deafening
St. John at Patmos

Vous descendez Madame?

QUI SOUVENT SE PESE BIEN SE CONNAIT
QUI BIEN SE CONNAIT BIEN SE PORTE

CONCORDE

I can't
I must go slowly

The   Tuileries   are   in   a   trance   20

because   the   painters   have

stared   at   them   so   long

Little boys in black overalls whose hands, sticky
with play, are like the newly furled leaves of
the horse-chestnuts ride round and round on
wooden horses till their heads turn.

                Pigeons perch on statues
                And are turned to stone.

        Le départ pour Cythère.

                These nymphs are harmless,   30
                Fear not their soft mouths –
        Some Pasteur made the Gauls immune
        Against the bite of Nymphs . . . look

                        Gambetta
        A red stud in the button-hole of his frock-coat
                The obscene conjugal *tutoiement*
                    Mais c'est logique.

        The Esprit Français is leaning over him,
                        Whispering
                          Secrets   40
                exquisite   significant
                    fade   plastic

                Of the XIIIth Duchess of Alba
                Long long as the Eiffel Tower
                Fathoms deep in haschich
                With languid compelling finger
                    Pointing invisible Magi
                To a little white Maltese:

                The back-ground gray and olive-green
                Like le Midi, the Louvre, la Seine. . . .   50

Of ivory paper-knives, a lion carved on the handle,
Lysistrata had one, but the workmanship of these is
Empire. . . .

            Of . . .

                I see the Arc de Triomphe,
        Square and shadowy like Julius Cæsar's dreams:
                Scorn the laws of solid geometry,
        Step boldly into the wall of the Salle Caillebotte
                    And on and on . . .

        I hate the Etoile
        The Bois bores me:

Tortoises with gem-encrusted carapace

A Roman boy picking a thorn out of his foot

  A flock of discalceated Madame Récamiers
  Moaning for the Chateaubriand *de nos jours.*

    And yet . . . quite near

  Saunters the ancient rue Saint-Honoré
Shabby and indifferent, as a Grand Seigneur from Brittany

An Auvergnat, all the mountains of Auvergne in
every chestnut that he sells. . . .

    Paris is a huge home-sick peasant,
    He carries a thousand villages in his heart.

      Hidden courts
With fauns in very low-relief piping among lotuses
    And creepers grown on trellises
Are secret valleys where little gods are born.

      One often hears a cock
Do do do miii

      He cannot sing of towns –
Old Hesiod's ghost with leisure to be melancholy
    Amid the timeless idleness of Acheron
    Yearning for 'Works and Days' . . . hark!

    The lovely Spirit of the Year
    Is stiff and stark

Laid out in acres of brown fields,

The crisp, straight lines of his archaic drapery
  Well chiselled by the plough . . .

And there are pretty things –
Children hung with amulets
Playing at *Pigeon vole*,   90
    Red roofs,
    Blue smocks,
And jolly saints . . .

                AU
          BON MARCHE
          ACTUELLEMENT
             TOILETTES
          PRINTANIERES

The jeunesse dorée of the sycamores.

In the Churches during Lent Christ and the Saints   100
are shrouded in mauve veils.

              Far away in gardens
                  Crocuses,
    Chionodoxa, the Princess in a Serbian fairy-tale,
                    Then
    The goldsmith's chef d'œuvre – lily of the valley,
                    Soon
Dog-roses will stare at gypsies, wanes, and pilgrimages

                All the time   110
            Scentless Lyons' roses,
                    Icy,
                  Plastic,
          Named after wives of Mayors. . . .

Did Ingres paint a portrait of Madame Jacquemart
André?

                In the Louvre
            The Pietà of Avignon,
                  L'Olympe,
                    Giles,   120
          Mantegna's Seven Deadly Sins,
                The Chardins;

They arise, serene and unetiolated, one by one from their subterranean sleep of five long years.

Like Duncan they slept well.

President Wilson grins like a dog and runs about the city, sniffing with innocent enjoyment the diluvial urine of Gargantua.

The poplar buds are golden chrysalids;
The Ballet of green Butterflies
Will soon begin.   130

During the cyclic Grand Guignol of Catholicism
Shrieks,
Lacerations,
Bloody sweat –
Le petit Jésus fait pipi.

Lilac

SPRING IS SOLOMON'S LITTLE SISTER; SHE HAS NO BREASTS.

LAIT SUPERIEUR
DE LA   140
FERME DE RAMBOUILLET

ICI ON CONSULTE
LE BOTTIN

CHARCUTERIE
COMESTIBLES DE I^{RE} CHOIX

APERITIFS

ALIMENTS DIABETIQUES
DEUIL EN 24 HEURES

Messieursetdames

PARIS: A POEM

        Little temples of Mercury;　　　　　　150
    The circumference of their *templum*
      A nice sense of scale,
  A golden drop of Harpagon's blood,
    Preserve from impious widening.

Great bunches of lilac among syphons, vermouth,
Bocks, tobacco.

    Messieursetdames

    NE FERMEZ PAS LA PORTE
      S. V. P.
    LE PRIMUS S'EN CHARGERA　　160

At marble tables sit ouvriers in blue linen suits discussing:

      La journée de huit heures,
      Whether Landru is a Sadist,
      The learned seal at the Nouveau Cirque
        Cottin. . . .

Echoes of Bossuet chanting dead queens.

      méticuleux
      bélligerants
      hebdomadaire
      immonde　　　　　　　　　　　170

    The Roman Legions
      Wingèd
      Invisible
Fight their last fight in Gaul.

    The ghost of Père Lachaise
      Is walking the streets,
He is draped in a black curtain embroidered with the
                letter H,
    He is hung with paper wreaths,
He is beautiful and horrible and the close friend of
      Rousseau, the official of the Douane.　　180

> The unities are smashed,
> The stage is thick with corpses. . . .

> Kind clever *gaillards*
Their *eidola* in hideous frames inset with the brass motto

> MORT AU CHAMP D'HONNEUR;
> And little widows moaning
> > Le pauvre grand!
> > Le pauvre grand!

And petites bourgeoises with tight lips and strident voices are counting out the change and saying *Messieursetdames* and their hearts are the ruined province of Picardie. . . .

They are not like us, who, ghoul-like, bury our friends a score of times before they're dead but –

> Never never again will the Marne
> Flow between happy banks.

It is pleasant to sit on the Grand Boulevards –
> They smell of
> > Cloacæ
> > Hot indiarubber
> > Poudre de riz
> > Algerian tobacco

Monsieur Jourdain in the blue and red of the Zouaves
> Is premier danseur in the Ballet Turque
> > 'Ya bon!
> > Mamamouchi

YANKEES – "and say besides that in Aleppo once . . ."
Many a *Mardi Gras* and *Carême Prenant* of the Peace Carnival;

> Crape veils,
Mouths pursed up with lip-salve as if they had just said:
> > *Cho - co - lat* . . .
> "Elles se balancent sur les hanches."

                    Lizard-eyes,
                    Assyrian beards,
                    Boots with cloth tops –

The tart little race, whose brain, the Arabs said, was
one of the three perches of the Spirit of God.

Ouiouioui, c'est passionnant – on en a pour son argent.
            Le fromage n'est pas un plat logique.

A a a a a oui c'est un délicieux garçon
Il me semble que toute femme sincère doit se retrouver
en Anna Karénine.

              Never the catalepsy of the Teuton
                    What time
                    Subaqueous
                    Cell on cell
                    Experience
                    Very slowly
                    Is forming up
              Into something beautiful – awful – huge

              The coming to . . . . . .
Thick halting speech – the curse of vastness.

                    The first of May
                         T
                         h
                         e
                         r
                         e

                         i
                         s

                         n
                         o

                         l
                         i
                         l

y

o

f

t
h
e

v
a
l
l
e
y

There was a ritual fight for her sweet body
    Between two virgins – Mary and the moon

    The wicked April moon.

    The silence of *la grève*

    Rain

    The Louvre is melting into mist

    It will soon be transparent
And through it will glimmer the mysterious island
gardens of the Place du Carrousel.

The Seine, old egotist, meanders imperturbably to-
                             wards the sea,

Ruminating on weeds and rain . . .
   If through his sluggish watery sleep come dreams
      They are the blue ghosts of king-fishers.

The Eiffel Tower is two dimensional,
Etched on thick white paper.

Poilus in wedgwood blue with bundles *Terre de Sienne*
are camping round the gray sphinx of the Tuileries.
They look as if a war-artist were making a sketch of
them in chalks, to be 'edited' in the Rue des Pyram-
ides at 10 francs a copy.

        Désœuvrement,   280
        Apprehension;
     Vronsky and Anna
Starting up in separate beds in a cold sweat
   Reading calamity in the same dream
    Of a gigantic sinister mujik. . . .

Whatever happens, some day it will look beautiful:
    Clio is a great French painter,
  She walks upon the waters and they are still.
Shadrach, Meshach, and Abednego stand motionless
                  and plastic mid the flames.

      Manet's *Massacres des Jours de Juin*,   290
       David's *Prise de la Bastille*,
        Poussin's *Fronde*,
        Hang in a quiet gallery.

   All this time the Virgin has not been idle;
The windows of les Galéries Lafayette, le Bon Marché,
                             la Samaritaine,
       Hold holy bait,
Waxen Pandoras in white veils and ties of her own
                                decking;
      Catéchisme de Persévérance,
The decrees of the Seven Œcumenical Councils re-
duced to the *format* of the *Bibliothèque Rose*,   300
       Première Communion,
  (Prometheus has swallowed the bait)
        Petits Lycéens,
       Por-no-gra-phie,
    Charming pigmy brides,
   Little Saint Hugh avenged –

     THE CHILDREN EAT THE JEW.

       PHOTO MIDGET

Heigh ho!
I wade knee-deep in dreams –

Heavy sweet going
As through a field of hay in Périgord.

The Louvre, the Ritz, the Palais-Royale, the Hôtel
de Ville
Are light and frail
Plaster pavilions of pleasure
Set up to serve the ten days junketing
Of citizens in masks and dominoes
A l'occasion du mariage de Monseigneur le Dauphin.

From the top floor of an old Hôtel,
Tranced,
I gaze down at the narrow rue de Beaune.
Hawkers chant their wares liturgically:
Hatless women in black shawls
Carry long loaves – Triptolemos in swaddling clothes:
Workmen in pale blue:
Barrows of vegetables:
Busy dogs:
They come and go.
They are very small.

Stories. . . .

The lost romance
Penned by some Ovid, an unwilling thrall
In Fairyland,
No one knows its name;
It was the guild-secret of the Italian painters.
They spent their lives in illustrating it. . . .

The Chinese village in a genius's mind. . . .

Little funny things ceaselessly happening.

In the Ile Saint-Louis, in the rue Saint Antoine, in the Place des Vosges
The Seventeenth Century lies exquisitely dying. . . .

Husssh

[musical notation: dim - in - u - en - do. ppp]

    In the parish of Saint Thomas d'Aquin there is
an alley called l'impasse des Deux Anges.

    Houses with rows of impassive windows;
        They are like blind dogs
    The only things that they can see are ghosts.   350
        Hark to the small dry voice
    As of an old nun chanting Masses
For the soul of a brother killed at Sebastopol. . . .

          MOLIERE
          EST MORT
        DANS CETTE MAISON
        LE 17 FEVRIER 1673

          VOLTAIRE
          EST MORT
        DANS CETTE MAISON   360
        LE 30 MAI 1778

       CHATEAUBRIAND
          EST MORT
        DANS CETTE MAISON
        LE 4 JUILLET 1848

        That is not all,
Paradise cannot hold for long the famous dead
                            of Paris. . . .
    There are les Champs Elysées!
Sainte-Beuve, a tight bouquet in his hand for Madame
                            Victor-Hugo,
Passes on the Pont-Neuf the duc de la Rochefoucauld   370
          With a superbly leisurely gait
          Making for the *salon d'automne*
          Of Madame de Lafayette;

They cannot see each other.

Il fait lourd,
The dreams have reached my waist.

We went to Benediction in Nôtre-Dame-des-Champs,
Droning... droning... droning.
The Virgin sits in her garden;
She wears the blue habit and the wingèd linen head-
dress of the nuns of Saint Vincent de Paul.
The Holy Ghost coos in his dove-cot.
The Seven Stages of the Cross are cut in box,
Lilies bloom, blue, green, and pink,
The bulbs were votive offerings
From a converted Jap.
An angelic troubadour
Sings her songs
Of little venial sins.
Upon the wall of sunset-sky wasps never fret
The plums of Paradise.

La Liberté La Presse!
La Liberté La Presse!

The sun is sinking behind le Petit-Palais.
In the Algerian desert they are shouting the Koran.

La Liberté La Presse!

The sky is apricot;
Against it there pass
Across the Pont Solférino
Fiacres and little people all black,
Flies nibbling the celestial apricot –
That one with broad-brimmed hat and tippeted pelisse
must be a priest.
They are black and two-dimensional and look like
silhouettes of Louis-Philippe citizens.

All down the Quais the bouquinistes shut their green boxes.

From the VIIme arrondissement

Night like a vampire
Sucks all colour, all sound.

The winds are sleeping in their Hyperbórean cave; 410
The narrow streets bend proudly to the stars;
From time to time a taxi hoots like an owl.

But behind the ramparts of the Louvre
Freud has dredged the river and, grinning horribly,
waves his garbage in a glare of electricity.

Taxis,
Taxis,
Taxis,

They moan and yell and squeak
Like a thousand tom-cats in a rut. 420
The whores like lions are seeking their meat from God:
An English padre tilts with the Moulin Rouge:
Crochets and quavers have the heads of niggers and
they writhe in obscene syncopation:
Toutes les cartes marchent avec une allumette!
A hundred lenses refracting the Masque of the Seven
Deadly Sins for American astigmatism:
"I dont like the gurls of the night-club – they love
women."
Toutes les cartes marchent avec une allumette! 430

DAWN

Verlaine's bed-time ... Alchemy
Absynthe,
Algerian tobacco,
Talk, talk, talk,
Manuring the white violets of the moon.

The President of the Republic lies in bed beside his
wife, and it may be at this very moment...
In the Abbaye of Port-Royal babies are being born,
Perhaps someone who cannot sleep is reading *le* 440
Crime et le Châtiment.
The sun is rising,

Soon les Halles will open,
The sky is saffron behind the two towers of Nôtre-
Dame.

JE VOUS SALUE PARIS PLEIN DE GRACE.

*
 *
*
   *   *
    * *

3 Rue de Beaune
Paris
Spring 1919

Notes

[The following are HM's own notes to *Paris*, printed in the Hogarth edition.]

Nord-Sud, one of the underground railways of Paris. *Dubonnet, Zig-zag, Lion Noir, Cacao Blooker* are posters. *Rue du Bac*, etc. are names of stations.

'It is pleasant to sit on the Grands Boulevards' to 'the curse of vastness' is a description of the Grands Boulevards.

'The first of May, there is no lily of the valley.' On May 1, the *Mois de Marie*, lily of the valley is normally sold in all the streets of Paris; but on May 1, 1919, the day of the general strike, no lily of the valley was offered for sale.

The April moon, *la lune rousse*, is supposed to have a malign influence on vegetation.

'The windows of *les Galéries Lafayette*, etc.' During Lent life-size wax dolls, dressed like candidates for Première Communion, are exposed in the windows of the big shops.

The Abbaye de Port-Royal is now a maternity hospital.

MOODS AND TENSIONS

Mothers

A mother sometimes dreams of an old age
Made safe and beautiful by her sons' swords,
And wind-proof by a daughter's spinning-wheel,
Reading from some obliterated page
The Protean future and its dubious awards,
Trying to stamp it with love's brittle seal.
For mothers fade, and she will have no part
In the Homeric laughter that she hears,
And, though she sees, she must ignore a daughter's tears,
Imprisoned in the ruined tower that is her heart.

The violet-scented fire-lit past is best.
That never hurts. A mother's memory
Marks, like a sundial, only sunny hours.
In that forsaken yet inviolable nest
Round which her dreams are fluttering ceaselessly
The little loves are playing among flowers –
Look how she laughs, *mater Cupidinum!*
Mater SAEVA *Cupidinum*, but with dove's eyes,
Guarding with flaming sword that Paradise
Which with the years her children's nursery has become.

Mothers are fierce, and we are lion's cubs.
There is a lion's cub in Aeschylus
That crouches in the logaoedic verse,
Rolls with the children in the dust, and rubs
Against the grandsire's sandals. Treacherous
And fawning little puss! It brought a curse,
The curse that Helen brought to Hector's kin,
Helen who lit the spark that burned down Troy.
The cub grew up to savage and destroy
The shepherd and his family who took it in.

But sometimes cubs can teach humility,
And then they bring a blessing to their dam,
Because she learns it, like the Saints, through love,
Through love and Simone Weil's necessity.
The lioness lies down beside the Lamb
In those green pastures that she told us of,
And we remain, seared by ingratitude.
But love lives on when those who loved are dead,
And we who gave our mother stones for bread
Still feel her bounty like a cloak or food.

The Copper-Beech in St. Giles' Churchyard

I walked along St. Giles, passing the golden doors
And the pale golden towers of St. John's,
Between the gold-flecked trunks of dappled sycamores
To evening Mass with summer at its height;
And on my way the beatniks and the dons
Seemed in the distance to be cast in bronze,
Embossed by the metállurgy of light;
And Advent seemed as far away as Lent,
For Church and trees since Whitsuntide had been
Enwrapped in vestments of a changeless green.
And gold idealized the Martyrs' Monument.

And in the churchyard where dim Georgians sleep
Leaving no trace on Oxford's halls or mart,
Whose head-stones look like little scabby sheep,
Rowlandson's ghost had put a touch of red
With true contrition and a hint of Goya's art.
For Rowlandson possessed a poet's heart,
And has learned pity now that he is dead.
So there where living tears no longer reach,
And village drabness is to gold immune,
And rustic psalmody is out of tune,
There grows among the graves a wine-red copper-beech.

And wrapped in gold I thought about my past,
And all the dreams that life has blown away,
And of uncovenanted joys that cannot last,
And of the place that made me what I am –
'Ye fields of Cambridge, our dear Cambridge, say
Have ye not seen us walking every day?'
The light blue flower that grows beside the Cam,
The turquoise of the past's forget-me-nots,
Is not found here. And yet the future's scent
Is sweet, stronger than disillusionment,
Though I await with trembling heart what it allots.

Hidden in time two various flowers perfume
Our hopes with the same scent. One flower, alas,
Is death; the other love. And either doom
Assails us old or young, early or late.
So as I sauntered through the gold to Mass
I wished I could decipher in a magic glass
What Oxford's dark blue flower is called, by fate.
And then I reached the church – an ugly place,
One to make Wren, but not the Angels, weep,
For here both Giles and John their vigil keep,
Although the gold is tinsel and the spire lacks grace.

And Oxford's homing pigeons haunt this church,
Some of them souls of the neglected folk
Whose graves I had just passed, and who now perch
Upon a Doom-Tree, like their own, wine-red.
No dying god hung on Dodona's oak
But when consulted long ago it spoke,
While birds foretell the future it is said.
And from *this* Tree the doves spoke thus: 'Dear friend,
We answer your heart's question: do not fear,
Love, only love, can be the answer *here*.
Take heart of grace, in your beginning is your end.'

July 1961

The Death of Cats and Roses

Did some old Chinese poet ever sing
The death of roses? Under one's very eye,
There, in the porcelain bowl, they curdle into art –
I have seen the profile of a Saxon king
Carved in a dying rose's ivory.
But dying roses never wring the heart,
Not even of a child...a rose is not a bird.
When he was put to sleep, I held my old cat, Maart,
And like Saint Simeon he was light with age,
But very warm, and I believe he purred.

Some drowsy power plays lazily with grief,
And makes rough patterns from life's poignancy,
As though an artist 'doodled' with his brush;
And seen in retrospect the pattern brings relief.
Maart's death has turned to macabre pot-pourri,
Because I stripped the roses from each bush
And lined a box with petals white and red,
Not hearing *then* the roses moralize,
And whisper that each living creature dies –
I was too busy making Maart a fragrant bed.

That rose-crowned poet, too, who strove in vain
To drown in temperate cups death's urgency,
Whose sacrificial kid for ever blends
Its blood with the pure spring, leaving no stain,
Enriched the pattern unobtrusively:
Horace's Odes, my old and kindly friends,
Were what I read while waiting for the bell,
But the well-tempered lyre was lost on me,
The pensive counterpoint and laughing Lalage,
Because I knew that I was waiting for Maart's knell.

§

It sounded, and my little cat is dead.
And she, who of Maart's love possessed the half,
The ordeal over, coined his epitaph:
'Maart died so gracefully', was what she said.

Envoy

In every cat a drop of rose-blood flows,
You surely must have seen an angry rose?
I have, and I could swear it spat!
A rose is just a vegetable cat –
Those lithe rose-withes that stretch and scratch your eyes!
Some enterprising florist should devise
A tiger-rose, for lilies have no thorns.
Yet for her cat this human-being mourns,
In spite of scratches from his loving claws,
Although of tears no rose can be the cause;
For if a poet weeps when a rose fades,
It is because he thinks of pretty maids.
Roses are symbols, and each rose that dies
Reminds us of the things they symbolize.
But Maart was nothing but a little cat,
And so I mourn *his* death, and only that.

A Skull

1

I wish my library had got a skull!
(All libraries should have *grave* furniture) –
Whose, whether that of poet, king or trull
Would not affect its erudite allure,
Like Latin in its logical bone-structure,
And which time's *accidence* cannot annul.

2

St. Jerome, in the wood-cut reassures
His study's fitness by a skull, and one
Lies in the closet where a dean endures
A lover's and a poet's doom – poor Donne!
Does Love's gold hair comfort his skeleton?...
Good God! Suppose the skull I owned was *yours*!

3

Beside the globe in its pale rosewood frame
Upon the Georgian table it would lie,
Saying, 'Remember that you too must die' –
Just that. And in the past did I not often blame
The coldness of the sculptured ivory,
The living eyes that never said my name!

4

But gazing on a skull resolves the stress
Of tuneless years in chords of baroque art,
Articulated richly to express
The grammar of assent learned by Mozart –
And suddenly my not unfaithful heart
Is sick with an unearthly tenderness.

Et in Arcadia Ego

I

I have no wish to eat forbidden fruit,
I did not gather roses when I might,
Now I am old and cold,
The years begin to turn on me and bite.
Nevertheless, replete and condescending queens,
Queens of the ants that drop their yellow wings,
Rich queens of diamonds on the *bridge* of sighs,
Doomed to a changeless menopause ennui,
However much you may despise,
You should not pity me –
I am Good Friday's child and have found fairy-gold,
I am bee-witched, gold-pollened with fern-seed,
I am a shepherdess and my flocks feed
On *Time*,
By the still waters of the past.
O the past's green pastures!

The apples never rot, no lily fades –
The past is Arcady.
I can watch the droves of little singing maids
(They are so close, *just* out of reach!)
Tuning Aeolian lyres upon the Lesbian beach,
And setting strange new songs to ancient airs;
And when the merry sea-bronzed fisher lads
Sway to the music, smile into their eyes,
O how that cloud of Cupid's butterflies,
The Cyprian's little doves,
Flattered and shy,
Daintily flutter, prettily twitter,
Behind their fingers rose-tipped like the Dawn's!
And their great mistress sits alone, and mourns.
And by my fire on cosy winter nights
I can watch Horace sipping his Sabine wine,
And smiling as he dreams of Nymphs and Fawns,
While Lydia plays soft airs upon her flute –
Spying on ghosts is *my* forbidden fruit!
And I know merry England too,
(Winged ants do you?)
Whenever I read Chaucer I smell May,
And I have milked the cows and tossed the hay
On little, secret, dung-sweet farms
Burned when the Roses rose in arms –
O the past's green pastures!

II

Why has it turned so cold, so Arctic cold?
Does Boreas blow in Arcady?
And in my haunted hospitable room
An uninvited spectre seems to loom,
That of an old and half-forgotten friend,
Whose lonely grave in Montparnasse,
Forsaken save by weeds and grass,
Long long ago I used to tend
With pious offerings of sombre dreams.
And now, sardonic, infinitely sad, he seems
To stand just here, beside my chair –
The weary, exiled ghost of Charles Baudelaire.

He too had been in Arcady (*had* been)!
Le paradis perdu des amours enfantines.
And then he spoke: –
'Who was the first to say "Et in Arcadia Ego?"
Ma pauvre semblable, *dare* you say his name?'
Dream-like, as from one hypnotized, my answer came:
'Death'.
Then cold and pitiful, like a faint breath
Of jonquils from a hearse in snow,
His words were slowly wafted, and he said:
'The great god Pan is dead,
As every poet ought to know.
The past is Arcady, and Arcady has passed.
The only flower in Arcady to last
Is the black-petalled tear-drenched lily, night.
Poor chatelaine of ghosts and shades!
Stealer of Virgil's vanished sheep!
Your only crops are dreams, your only sheaves.
Títyrus, and Amaryllis sleep.'
And in my ears the eerie voice still sings.
Then under the electric light
I saw a sallow vitreous heap
Of sodden, trodden, frost-nipped willow leaves. . .
Or were they just an insect's fallen wings?

The Land of Uz

There was a man in the land of Uz whose name was Job.

At last the thing we feared has come on us,
Because an Angel seized us by the hair
When we were unaware,
And dropped us in the hideous land of Uz.
Yes, we have come.
Here, friends are cold as fishes, but not dumb –
They moralize;
And some of them are happy little birds,
Who from the withered hedgerows sing to us

Gay little songs with very trivial words
That tell of warmth, and worms, and flies,
Hidden by March behind its turquoise skies;
Not of the cloudy treacheries of snow,
Although
This is the land of horrible surprise,
This is the land of Uz –
Poor foolish, egotistic little birds!
And blessings here seem ministers of hate,
Goblins of hell that mop and mow,
Shrieking 'You fools, too late, too late!'
The thriving of his scrannel flocks and herds
Deepens the mourning farmer's woe,
Foison is poison here,
For love lies cold upon the bier;
And in the agonizing Keats's ear
The honeyed joys now buzz
With waspish ironies –
This is the mocking land of Uz. . .
And yet, in gentler climates memories
From their long summer's sleep will rise again
Not without pain,
For their unaltered tenderness will hurt –
These memories of April's rain-washed sweets;
But not as here, ah not as *here*!
To tortured genius in the dark, like Keats,
The past is Heracles's poisoned shirt –
This is the ghastly land of Uz.
And as for us, poor pain-besotted us,
We grow ungrateful and cantankerous,
And think that those we love give us short measure,
And whine like beggars and stretch out our hands
With angry piteous demands,
Not for a beggar's dole
But for the vast and undivided whole
Of their hearts' buried dedicated treasure –
This is the greedy land of Uz.
And what of God? God is the duke who left his folk
To rot in chains under the devil's yoke,
The devil whom he chose as deputy
That he himself might play a dubious role,
And secretly pursue his devious ways.

Nevertheless. . .
Did the great nameless poet have the key
To his stupendous tragi-comedy
Composed by starlight in the dim old days,
To all its searchings of the soul,
To all its dark perplexity?
How could he *then* have found the key?
He knew that Job must kiss the rod.
He could not guess that Job himself was God.
This is Gethsemane.

The Glass Tánagra

I dreamt that I had wandered far away
To landscapes that were alien and rococo,
And knew that I was living long ago
For Wedgwood had just started 'throwing clay'.
But in my dream the fashion of the day
Were tánagras that Nereids might blow
From moonlight, foam, and sunsets at Murano,
And one small chef-d'oeuvre filled me with dismay.
And as I watched what seemed my tears roll down
The spotless uncreased drapery of glass,
Making it shine like dew on summer grass,
In sudden rage I smashed it with a stone.
And then I heard the gentle Petrarch moan,
'The broken thing is her own heart, alas!'

The Legend of the Painted Room

If poets are to win to artistry
They first must learn to model beauty out of tears,
And only if their heart-strings are left free
To winds that blow harsh airs discordantly
Can poets learn Aeolian melody.
And who are we that we should blame

These martyrs of Apollo if they claim
The pagan poet's solace – love and wine?
Hidden in Oxford is 'the painted room',
A vintner's once, whose wife was beautiful;
And in this vintner's tavern, Stratford-bound,
Shakespeare would break his journey, so they say,
And I believe.
And in the painted room he would receive
Refreshment from the dusty work-a-day
In wine and beauty – both divinely cool.
Three friends (I now am speaking of to-day):
The wife of a great poet lately dead,
(A poet who had long endured
A semi-mystical, Arthurian wound
From an Archangel's spear, which she had cured)
Next, a small creature, patient, humble, dumb;
Myself the third, stood in that 'painted room'
Where the great, storm-tossed poet found
The bitter-sweet viaticum
Of Horace and Anacreon.
A pencil-stub too blunt to mark,
A clock with damaged chimes,
A match too damp to strike – so seems
My sensibility at certain times:
And when the present will not light
The past stays dark –
Clio (who is my Muse) has docked my dreams,
I felt in that historic room that I had lost
My meagre visionary powers,
For *even* Prospero's magic had not tricked
My docile fancy into seeing a ghost.
And for my friend, I wondered if her thoughts
Were with *il miglior fabbro*, or her own.
But we were three. What of two little ears,
Soft, black and pricked,
Of two eyes, round and goblin-bright,
Eyes phosphorescent – innocent
As are the golden eyes of certain small spring flowers?
My little dog, although debarred
From 'intellectual good', perhaps has heard
The Swan of Avon singing a madrigal,
Perhaps he has *seen* the Bard!

'Une Maison Commode, Propre, et Belle...'

A well-found house, commodious, sweet, and clean,
A wholesome diet cooked with careful skill,
The smiling service of complete good-will,
Peace, roses, and the fairy-gift of green
From sheltering trees, my bed-room's joy and screen,
No children and no debts my sleep to kill,
And Bach's divine good-sense my fears to still –
Such are the blessings of the golden mean
Which in His goodness God vouchsafes to me,
The pleasant, peaceful things of Plantin's prayer,
And I am grateful. None the less I dare
To beg a far more costly gift of Thee,
A pearl, great God, from the Saints' treasury –
Patience, the only nostrum for despair.

The Rendez-Vous

Quaerens me sedisti lassus

The sultry scene by Jacob's well when Christ
Sat waiting in the heat for one who came,
Unwitting and unawed, to keep the tryst
(And you shall later learn her name)
Dogma permits with equal truth to be portrayed
By the dramatic art of Rembrandt's light and shade,
(Mellow with ripeness of a sun
That will inevitably fade),
As one unique historic day;
Or in the cold, Byzantine, hieratic way
Sub specie aeternitatis.
She was no matron of established worth,
She was a common woman of ill-fame,
A woman who was neither maid nor wife,
A light o' love, and yet her mystic fate is

To be the prototype of everyone
At the decisive moment of his life:
Of Rochester, Paul Claudel, you and me,
St. Bernadette, St. Catherine of Siena –
Which helps to teach us all humility.
So either in the chiaroscuro of To-day,
Or stylized in mosaics of Ravenna
The scene can be depicted and be true.

She plodded to the fated rendez-vous
Through heat and dust, and when at last she met
Her Master by the well she did not disobey
The common evangelical vocation –
She found Him thirsty and she gave Him drink.
Each Gospel episode and every link
In the redemptive chain 'twixt Heaven and earth
While taking place
In time and space
Conceals an anagogic explanation.
The name is PSYCHE of this unrefined
And untaught woman of Samaria,
And He was waiting at the well for all mankind.
The well can be a burning-bush in the Sahara –
The rendez-vous need not be at Sichāra.
For me it was in Paris thirty-odd years ago
At the collected paintings of Berthe Morisot.

Bertha frightens Miss Bates

Fresh, smiling, and domestic as a rose,
Varnished and shining from the April rain,
The red brick ripe, but not yet stained by time,
Regency houses built in honeyed prose,
Some timbered cottages in Chaucer's rhyme –
The little town, so seemly and so sane
Was like a timeless picture by Vermeer.
But down the High Street sped 'a maiden fair',
And though her bonnet and sprigged-muslin gown

Might have been bought at Fords in their own town,
Yet all the passers-by stopped open-mouthed to stare:
'Lord love a duck!' they cried, 'No Miss like she lives *here*.'

The French, some said, must be about to land,
And doubtless this strange lass was Boney's spy,
And all agreed her eyes were sly and wild;
Little John Knightley clutched Aunt Emma's hand
And wondered if it was a *fairy's* child;
The two Miss Coxes tittered *'What* a guy!'
But no one guessed that drowsy honey cates,
And eerie things, half ballad and half flower,
Meadowsweet, lords and ladies, passion fruit,
The deadly nightshade and the insane root,
Such things as grow and twine in Proserpina's bower,
Were in a basket she was taking to Miss Bates.

She said, 'I'm Bertha from the Minster Square'.
And as she quietly shut the parlour door
All seemed to turn into a Gothic book –
Dumbfounded, poor Miss Bates could only stare,
Her good old mother in the chimney-nook
Grinned like a witch, and polly turned macaw.
'So kind!' she gasped, 'I cannot quite recall...'
Then through the room a scent spread like a stain,
And cosy pussy on the worsted mat
Became 'a silken-haired Angora cat',
And last – the parlour's heart, the crayon sketch of Jane,
With sudden catastrophic thud fell from the wall.

On this the visitor intently gazed:
'Yes, it is she – the pale cheek, the grey eye!'
And all at once the little room turned dark.
'Listen!' she said. So, trembling and amazed,
Miss Bates was told the legend of St. Mark,
And how those doomed within the year to die,
At dusk upon the vigil of his feast
Fluttered like moths into the minster church,
And Bertha watching saw among the crowd
The lady of the portrait in her shroud,
Who ere another spring breathed green upon the birch
Would have no further need of lover, leech, or priest.

Then, like a wraith herself, she slipped away,
And cheerful noises could be heard again,
And all was just as it had been before,
No homely parlour could have looked less fey,
And Bertha might have never crossed the door.
So our poor friend, still sobbing, 'My *dear* Jane!'
Put the drugged buns into a biscuit-tin
As supper for herself and Mrs. Bates;
And with the first taste, prophecies of woe
Melted as magically as April snow.
While seeing that the ladies duly paid their rates,
The eerie flowers were thrown into the dustman's bin.

But some of them were blown through Highbury,
Which put the light of reason in eclipse:
Poor Mr. Woodhouse had disturbing dreams
And woke up screaming and demanding Perry;
Elton, abandoning his usual themes,
That Sunday preached from the Apocalypse;
The children found a fair in Donwell Wood,
With real winged horses for the roundabout;
One pint of beer made William Larkins tipsy,
And Harriet dreamt young Martin was a gipsy.
Emma alone ignored the Comus-rout,
And blamed 'the blackthorn winter' for the foolish mood.

Envoy

A vestal virgin serving the domestic hearth,
Calm and ironic, a Jane Austen heroine,
Armed with the *Rambler* and *The Book of Common Prayer*,
Passes inviolate the fairies in her path:
The dragon *and* St. George, Sirens, Balder the Fair.
Pitted against our dreams strong prose will often win;
But mightier than prose glitters Excalibur.
In eighteenth-century divines the ore is found
Wrought by Jane Austen to a perfect instrument –
A conscience exquisitely poised. And this she lent
To Emma, whom it made not merely sane and sound,
But pure enough to wear, one day, the Morning Star.

In a Pagan Wood

At times in the post-prandial solitude
Of one of Oxford's ancient College-halls
I sit, a renegade, at the high-table
On afternoons with summer's gold imbrued;
My only company the portraits on the walls
Of silenced clerics and quenched legal-lights,
Who yawn through unconvivial gaudy nights,
A band of listless melancholy ghosts
Too dull for speeches and too sad for toasts.
Yet, harmless though they seem, I feel afraid,
As did the Greeks at high noon in a forest glade.
Perhaps the grave is *not* a quiet bed,
And even ghosts of dons are nymphs and fauns,
Animulae, versed in all Jungian tricks,
Their learning nothing else but swaddling clothes,
Their strict decorum just a cap and gown
To be discarded when the body goes.
So cloven hooves imprint the College-lawns
And voices can be heard singing to drown
Old colleagues in the waters of the Styx.

Yes, College-halls, I think, are fairy woods,
Perhaps the forest which we call the Past,
Which traps secure in *camera obscura*
The light and shade of Oxford's shifting moods,
And where phenomena for ever last:
Fruit carved by Grinling Gibbons ripens on trees,
Snow lies that fell in Tudor days, and bees
Rob flowers to sweeten Burton's surly tongue,
While branches net the moon that Sidney sung,
And *all* the poets are immortal in the thrush.

Then, when there comes a sudden pregnant hush
And a faint scent of blubells and dead leaves,
Down alleys tiptoes past the ghosts of Pater.
Ευφημε ω χρη. How should I dare to speak,
A stranger in these woods frozen with fear,
Not of the *incubi* of Jungian fable

But of the 'Gracious One' they worship here,
Their dark blue mother-goddess, Alma Mater?
And yet this Cambridge dunce at the high-table
Knows that at least to-day she is an ancient Greek.

Sickness and Recovery at the Cape of Good Hope in Spring

I

There's nothing lovelier than the Cape in spring,
When winter rains have turned it gold and green –
Green veld, green vines, gold of Australian wattle,
And of the tree that bears the golden brush
To clean the broken, green, glass bottle
From which Silvanus quaffs his kaffir-beer,
Silvanus of the velt, the *braak*, the bush,
Whose Tuscan tan the sun is burning black.
There's nothing lovelier than the spring in *lente*,
The time when birds are flow'rs with wings,
The time when every flower sings –
Hark to the sudden burst of freesia-scent!
And nowhere else but in the Cape in spring
Can one enjoy the sweet incongruous sight
Of herds of pretty Jersey cows
Feeding among lilies like the Shunamite,
An arum-egret on each lady's back.
And mark the gum-trees' sculptured boughs,
And listen to the Latin of the doves,
The pigeon-Latin of the doves who sing
An ode of Horace about love and spring:
'Sáy it with flów'rs, sáy it with flów'rs,
Say it with flów'rs, Léukonoé.'
How wise are doves and Horace, O how wise!
And watch the troops of Coloured *Meisies*,
Who trip like dusky Primaveres
Among the gold of the Namaqua daisies,
Skirting 'the quaint enamelled eyes'

Of jewelled multi-coloured *vagies*
Carrying sheaves
Of poinsettia's scarlet leaves,
And with the chic of the O.K. Bazaar
Looking themselves like gaudy flow'rs –
Ben Jonson's *Masque of Blackness* in fresh guise!
The vision from which Gauguin learned his art!
Yes, many a sight to dazzle and surprise
A visitor from quiet skies
Is to be found on all roads and at all hours.
Yet there are times when I have seen the Cape
Dishevelled, wild and panting from the rape
Of the marauding Viking waves
That ride on the Atlantic ocean,
Her willing arms loaded with foreign gifts!
Her roses, and her northern trees,
Her pines and vines and pungency
And the cool nights of 'Overseas',
Are gifts from the Atlantic breeze.
And now and then in her full radiant year
You'll find her sitting pensive by the shore,
Recalling centuries that are no more,
Or haunted by some cosmic fear;
And her eternal background is austere –
Those touching mountains, old and low and grey,
Patiently burdened with ancestral grief:
A granite Graeco-Indian frieze
Of overlapping elephants in low relief,
Carved with a line as sharp and clear
As that of stars in this pure hemisphere.
But see!
The sky is 'turning' like an autumn tree,
It turns and burns
Lime-yellow, poplar-gold, and maple-red,
A sky from which at any moment on your head,
With crushing thunderous impact,
A giant Tintoretto saint might hurtle down...
But what is this? Ah me! alack!
Surely the omens frown?
The birds against that painted sky look black.
The Greeks read omens from the flight of birds,
Mark well that sable *cortège* and beware!

For now the mountains are about to act,
In colours more significant than words,
The changeless ritual of their parts
In their old sunset-tragedy:
They fall in love, then mourn their love, then die.
So *sursum corda* and prepare
To watch them hierophantically disclose
The story carved on their primeval hearts.
At first they turn a wild celestial rose,
And then a purple, deep and rich as Brahms,
Then hopelessly they wither back to grey,
Not blessèd twilight-grey that soothes and charms
Sun-wearied eyes and aching head,
But dreary, lifeless grey – the grey of lead.
Nature! Begin your threnody,
The mountains of the Cape are dead.

II

I was dead too not very long ago.
To sleep, some say, is to forestall
The sleep of death, but now I know
It is not sleep that is death's counterpart
But sickness which has lost the gift of dreams.
The day I drove to the Volkshospitaal,
Although the journey lay through golden fires,
And past the Cape's Renaissance themes,
(The black nymphs dressed like gaudy flowers,
The mountains' Botticelli-line)
Not one of them was mine;
For ghosts no longer have a share
In the sweet upper air –
'Nothing we see in nature that is ours'.
But did a bird or poet ever sing
A doleful ending to a song of spring?
For spring is nature's 'Joyful Mystery',
A miracle, and worked this time for *me*.
And though my grateful heart is fain
To give to God the thanks that are His due,
Yet I have set them to a pagan strain.
For without doubt my chequered story

Of ancient gods, of stars and trees,
Of sunset's flowers and vanished glory,
Marauding waves and sundering seas,
Of stalking terror and escape,
Of iridescent rain and shine,
Mountains that mourn and Hell that laughs,
Describes in nature's pictographs
The flower-crowned Earth-child's cyclic rape,
The dreams and the autumnal tears
Of ravished Proserpine.
And tell how prowling through the riant Spring
A scout of Hades seized me from behind
And looked at me and set me free –
I was too old to be Persephone!

Winter Trees

In that elusive hour that comes between
The setting of the winter sun and night,
I contemplate a line of tall, thin, trees,
Black crotchets, strong and perpendicular,
Played by wood-winds, inaudibly, bat-high;
Black with a blackness absolute yet manifold,
Like veils of Vestal Virgins tending the evening star;
Taciturn and indifferent donors of delight,
Silent and self-absorbed, they stand
Against the violet, vitreous, winter sky
That greyly recreates a half-remembered blue.
There is a T'ang about this English scene,
A T'ang mysteriously Japanese:
Not kittens sleeping among peonies,
Or decorations on a Kano screen
Painted in autumn colours upon gold;
One medium only could attempt to catch
Those sable nuances just barely seen,
That blackness absolute yet manifold –
The subtly graded shades of *suiboku* ink
Turned to unfading beauty by Sesshu.

And what but *suiboku* ink could match
That violet sky of half-remembered blue?
And sometimes as the dusk draws on I think
That from my bedroom window I can see
The painter-priest of Zen, the saffron robed Sesshu,
In mystic contemplation on my lawn
Gazing in rapture at my winter trees,
Less conscious than are they of time and place
And whether he is dead or not yet born;
Seeking to find a pattern, and thus earn,
If not 'Enlightenment', a painter's peace.
But by what branch of trigonometry
Could even Leonardo hope to trace
The angles of the crossing twigs and boughs?
Or hear the crotchets of the quavering tune?
Apollo, god of pattern, could not snatch
His Daphne from a tree's complexities!
And who can find the lost or hidden clue
That will unravel all the wavering lace?
Not Argus, not the venom-sharpened eye
Of the owl-goddess, wide-awake with spleen
Through deadly envy of an insect's skill.
Nevertheless, gaze on my trees, Sesshu,
Gaze long and take your fill!
Failure is golden, as great Rysdael knew,
Who gave to woods Rembrandt's significance
And Virgil's *chiaroscuro* to his native sky.
And thus with poetry, he would enhance,
Not try to solve, the mystery of the *seen*;
For were that mystery solved, then art would die.
But for the painter-priest this was not all
That caused the torment of the soul and eye –
There was the anguish of the ephemeral.
And hence these mystically aesthetic men
Would laugh (a little wryly) at the moon,
And, in defiance of their love of flowers,
Banish the Ballet of the Hours
From gardens made of rocks and sand.
And that is why,
Despite the migratory evening sky,
I sometimes think that I can see Sesshu
Gazing in rapture at my winter trees.

And on this quiet evening, save when fanned
By a small, feeble, intermittent breeze
As by the languid and reluctant hand,
Half-hidden in the mists of Murasaki's sleeves,
Of a dead lady from Kyoto's vanished Court,
For hours on end they seem to stand
As still as if they also had been taught
Pure contemplation in a school of Zen.
Are winter trees invulnerable, then?
Immune from all the changes that we mean
By anguish of the ephemeral?
The fatal predetermined fall
Of dedicated death-struck leaves?
The cyclic treachery of green?
Like soughing ghosts of Nho
The autumns of the future murmur 'No'.

§

But dusk is darkening upon this half
Of the terrestrial globe, and soon
We shall not see a single tree
In English gardens or in Old Japan.
So let us, therefore, Sesshu san,
Gaze at the *moon* –
And laugh!

A Portrait of the Second Eve, Painted in Pompeian Red

(The so-called Villa dei Misteri *on the outskirts of Pompeii is noted for its series of frescoes depicting the initiation rites of the Roman Mysteries of Bacchus, Mysteries to which only women were admitted. One of the frescoes is known as 'The frightened lady'* (La donna atterrita)*, of which the subject is a candidate for initiation confronted by the terrifying spectacle of a black-winged being holding a whip in his upraised hand, and evidently about to flagellate a naked young woman lying prone at his feet. The double purpose of these Mysteries was to render the neophytes both fruitful and holy – among the sacred objects of the cult a phallus is unmistakeably depicted. The final fresco is of 'the frightened lady' dancing the ritual dance of a fully initiated and hence fully sanctified Bacchante. The frescoes are believed to have been commissioned by the chatelaine of the* Villa, *herself an initiate and a priestess of Bacchus.)*

Because the story of an Angel sent
To warn a Hebrew maiden full of Grace
Of what God held for her in store,
Namely a weight of Glory so immense
As to appal and freeze the mortal sense,
Is true in poetry as well as true in fact,
It can occur both after and before
The one unchangeable and strict event;
Hence the terrestrial scene of this great act,
The little house with Angels at the door,
Is found in any age and any place –
In Galilee or in Pompeii
Or even in a city of the plain,
If love lives on in spite of pain;
And on the flaky gesso of the wall
The future's indecipherable script
And faded frescoes of the past depict
A message different yet the same for all.
There is a picture I would like to trace,
Restored from the apocrypha of dreams,
In garish colours of . . . a heresy?
Look! To the frightened maiden full of Grace,
And, in a figure, to the lady from Pompeii,
The 'frightened lady' who for Grace is seeking

In the predestined house, soon Death's escheat,
The Bacchic *Villa dei Misteri*,
A Messenger from Heaven holds out a fruit,
And of their courtesy invites them both to eat.
But then the shadows of the room take shape
And seem to be a horror of black wings,
A horror which to both of them is speaking
In broken music of a voice once sweet:
'Mothers to be! Have pity on the race,
Save it O save it from the doom
Of endless sufferings heaped on sufferings.
I solemnly adjure you *Do not eat*,
For what he offers you is – Passion fruit;'
And every word he utters pierces their womb.
And then the *donna atterrita*
Cowers and hides her face and screams,
But the Angelic Messenger stands mute.
And in a flash the timid questionings
Troubling the Flow'r of Time, the Maid of Grace
Are silenced once for all, and looking up
Into the Angel's quiet impenetrable face,
'The Will of God', she says, 'is surely sweeter
Than any of my foolish wayward dreams,
Give me the fruit and I will gladly eat.'
At that the Angel cries in a great voice
Reaching to both Time's silent banks:
'Years that seem dead and years unborn give thanks
And call this Maiden blessed!
Sad stars of destiny rejoice!
Clash your gold cymbals now and sing,
For, Mary, you have chosen well.
I am God's messenger, my name is Gabriel,
The Angel of the true Annunciation,
No mortal man escapes from suffering,
The pain *I* offer you bears fruit,
He is the lord of evil flagellation,
Who offers you the fruitless pain of hell.'

Amor Fati

God wrote His holy laws on stars and stones.
We break the stones at will. No man can mar
An adamant irrefragable star.
In stars a loving Seraph ever moans –
Yet stalks us like a tiger, one by one
Through all the dubious mansions of the sun.

The weeping Seraph in the stars is Fate,
And Fate commands our love, the Stoics taught.
This means I must love *you*, though I have fought
To wrest morose delight from lovelorn hate
For one who blazes in my horoscope,
But in whose own no star foretells this HOPE.

Heaven is Not Fairyland

Heaven is not Fairyland (alas!)
This world seen in a magic glass;
Gingerbread houses but without the witch;
The joyful bark of my dead dachshund bitch;
A glut of carbo-hydrates that never make you fat –
No, Heaven, they say, is *not* like that.
The holy souls, like the Angelic nation
Have neither senses nor imagination;
While pierced by intellect and pulverized by fact,
All dreams expire in God, Pure Act.
God, God, God, nothing but God! How can we stand it?
We can't as yet, I fear, but when we've safely landed
We may find Fairyland, with all its tales come true,
Lying quite close to walk into.
The happy ending of an old *love*-story
Is what is meant, the Saints have found, by Glory.

Gulls

The Protestants lie safe and snug in bed,
Unharassed by the voracious dead.
But till our scruples saving reason lulls
Our sleep is torn by flocks of screaming gulls;
Not the familiar souls of those one loves,
(They are as gentle and as tame as doves,
A welcome flock that without clamour comes
Morning and evening for the scattered crumbs),
But souls of those met once, or long ago,
Who haunt the only Catholics they know,
Shrieking and wailing: 'Friend, throw us a crust,
A *Pater*, or an *Ave* for the love of Christ!
To none but papists can we go for meat,
Pity the poor prisoners of the Fleet.'
And I remember how our gallant dead
Who lost their lives in the two wars are fed –
They give them poppies when they ask for bread.

A Meditation on Donatello's Annunciation in the Church of Santa Croce, Florence

I

The rosary's First Joyful Mystery
Plyed in the marble of a high-relief
Is ravishing but odd.
The lady looks affronted, and one might suppose
Some humble suppliant by terror rendered bold,
(Terror of death or urgency of grief)
Stealthily slipping through the palace gates
Had ventured to invade her private enfilade;
And judging by her angry and forbidding look
Her thoughts are very far from God.
But patiently the humble suppliant waits –

A very strange Annunciation!
And though the lady holds a book,
One knows without so much as glancing at a page
It is no Psalter and no Book of Hours,
But it might well be the *Decamerone*.
And mark the pretty tracery
Of shell-like leaves and stylized flow'rs
Upon the moulded panels of the wall,
Nature subdued and tamed,
Gilded and gelt for decoration,
The emblems of an artificial age
And of a brittle civilization,
(Heian Japan or ancient Crete)
Which serve as an unwritten inventory
Of the rich ornaments in some palatial room,
Easily pictured although they are not named.
Note too the art which makes the marble show
The texture of the rich patrician gown
Hanging in many a classic fold,
The work of some Venetian loom.
And see! The background is all flecked with gold,
But not with gold-leaf from the sunset trees
Of Angel-haunted groves in Paradise
That falls upon the brush of Fra Angelico,
This is the golden rain of Midas or of Danaë.
And as one looks it almost could be said
The lady's marble cheek was turning red,
(For a great sculptor sometimes can endue
His marble with rose's native blush
As though his chisel were Giorgione's brush)
Not the same blush that Gabriel *really* saw,
The blush of wonder and of awe
That turned a lily to a rose,
And never fades from Mary's cheek,
For being flesh and blood she still can blush,
And though the Queen of Heaven, she still is meek.
The blush upon the haughty lady's cheek
In this great quattrocento portraiture,
Only to art and outraged pride is due;
Or else she has been taken unaware
Drying the waves of her close crisped hair
Before a fire made fragrant with the scent

MOODS AND TENSIONS

Of cedar-wood, and of some precious grains
Of special incense, as a tribute sent
By some obsequious cleric of the papal court.
And patiently the suppliant she disdains,
Kneels humbly and implores –
No, the poor suppliant *adores*,
And in that word 'adores' there lies
The marble group's anomaly.
Madonna tell, Madonna tell, O
Donna tell Renaissance-dazzled Donatello
You are not named Lucrezia d'Este,
Yours is a bidding name – it is ADESTE.

II

But what of the Angel? What of St. Gabriel?
Because they would not serve the Angels fell;
And then through all the heavenly mansions burst
A polyphonic music of assent:
'We will serve, obey, pay homage and adore,'
From Cherubim and Seraphim and many a score
Of the Angelic hosts who with their glittering swords,
By valour tempered, damascened with faith,
Routed the legions led by Lucifer,
Legions forlorn who threw away their shields,
Legions accursed.
The music trembled through the lower skies
And rained down melody on summer fields,
Then scattering stars of clarion harmonies
(Of which a few still sparkle, I surmise,
In Purcell's golden trumpet rhapsodies)
It thundered down to the abyss
Where envy and self-pity rent
The merciless and iron bowels of hell,
Because the tortured diabolic hordes
Knew well
Just what that joyful arioso meant,
That polyphonic music of assent
And that the wielders of the fatal swords
Were now eternally confirmed in bliss.
For Angels and Archangels know

This mighty *Wheel* which is the *Will* of God
Must be the *weal* of Angels and of men,
Because the linch-pin of the Wheel is love.
The faces of the dead are nature's works of art,
Stamped with the peace of impassivity
That comes when wills have ceased to operate,
And when no longer in the tortured heart
The suffocating passions throb and pulsate.
But Donatello has imbued the face
Of Gabriel with a *living* peace,
The still-life of a flower whose will is God's.
'For of their will Angels make sacrifice
To God, singing *Hosanna.*'
Here is the sweetness born when envy dies,
The candour shining from the single-eyed,
The gentleness that only is distilled
From crushed and trampled pride;
For in these marble features is fulfilled
The beauty that the Angels share with Saints,
The Saints who like the Angels feed on Manna.
And hence he *kneels* before his future Queen,
Whose portrait once was seen
By yet a greater Florentine
Carved on the marble wall of Purgatory,
With deeper faith than nature can command,
And greater art than that of ancient Greece –
Almost the sculpture of a voice
Articulating the momentous choice,
Those humble words by which would be restored
To fallen men both love and peace:
'Behold the handmaid of the Lord,
Be it unto me according to thy word.'
And so it was that when the Angel's glance,
Grown eagle-keen from gazing at the Sun,
First fell upon the pure and lowly maid
He saw at once her full significance,
And that the treacherous goddess of the sea,
To whom in her intact, and therefore perfect, ode
With burning faith the Lesbian prayed,
Imploring the specific sovereign boon
For which wild hearts have ever yearned,
The boon that love may be returned,

MOODS AND TENSIONS

Was other than she seemed to be.
For pious Sappho was undone
Because she lacked the urge to seek the One,
And yet possessed the gift of the green sight
Which sees Nymphs dancing under the moon.
And though he prudently avoids her name,
Yet Horace in a famous ode,
The lovely ode to Pyrrha,
Warns us against the Cyprian and her wiles
By many a half concealed allusion,
In ordered metrical confusion
Between the winds and sea, Venus and Pyrrha;
And each keeps merging with, dissolving into each
Until at last one scarcely knows
Which one he means, and which is which,
Or whether each one is the same:
We know that from the sea the Cytherean rose,
And wiles are woven too by Pyrrha,
And winds blow when and where they choose,
And mariners and lovers should beware
Of smiling seas and smiles of the Fair,
For golden weather will not last,
And smiles of golden girls are quickly overcast,
And when the white and vitreous sea
Is smooth as Venus' golden mirror
All of a sudden winds will bark and roar,
And then the sea will bare her dragon's teeth
(The dragon's teeth that Juno may have sowed
To wreck Ulysses homeward bound)
And mariners and lovers are no more,
For in the tangled waves of seas or golden hair
Poor lovers and poor mariners are drowned;
Because the Cyprian and the sea, the winds and Pyrrha
Are symbols both of love and death –
So intricate and subtle is this famous ode!
But the Archangel as he kneels perceives
That it was not the treacherous sea
But *Maris Stella*, the sea's star,
Whom Sappho without knowing it implored,
For stars are 'steadfast'.
And that, by myths of man for long concealed,
The pagan mother-goddess stands revealed

As mirror both of mercy and of truth
In whom can be no shadow of deception,
The dark, chaotic, treacherous *Anima*
Made pure and luminous at last –
Mary, the Immaculate Conception,
No goddess, but the Virgin Mother of God's Love.
It was to *her* that the Archangel kneeled –
But also he adored. . .
In that appalling scene enacted in his cell
Between an odious father and a graceless son,
Before the shocked spectators of a total loss
Of self-respect and human dignity,
And its wild climax Father Zossima fell
In veneration, prostrate at the feet
Of the outrageous son, Dimitri Karamazov,
Because with saintly prescience he foresaw
The frightful doom of suffering in store
For that poor sinner – and St. Gabriel,
Kneeling before the Maid, adores the Cross.
Madonna tell, Madonna tell, O
Donna tell the Catholic-nurtured Donatello
He must have *seen* St. Gabriel.

A Doggerel Epitaph for My Little Dog, Sally

Here lies the dust of my small peke.
She had no need to learn to speak,
For tongues will sometimes tell you lies,
But *never* will a doggy's eyes.
She had no need of printed book,
For she could read my every look.
She owned but little: harness, ball,
Her basket and my heart, that's all.
And if I hear in death's dark valley
A distant bark, I'll know it's Sally.

Jesus Wept

My mother had a maid called Barbara,
And she was born under a tragic star,
But no one ever saw her shed a tear,
For she was crowned with love, as was Queen Guinevere.

For love she drowned herself, and she was held accurst.
To pray for her gentle nor simple durst,
And through the timeless years of poetry she slept
Unmourned and unannealed, but Jesus wept.

PREVIOUSLY UNPUBLISHED POEMS
AND TRANSLATIONS

I'd like to get into your dreams

He said: 'I'd like to get into your dreams.'
   To lovers tired with making love it seems
     That lying side by side asleep
   Fulfils the joys of their relationship:
     Twins in the womb, birds in the nest,
       Intimacy at its safest and best;
But one is travelling east, the other west,
     And they are stars apart –
As are our beds. But when full fathom five
   You lie in sleep, I want to dive
Into your dreams, and there I'll find your heart.

Crossed in Love

for V.E.

Is it presumptuous to suppose that love
Is only given by God to planet Earth?
Well, it's a boon of which we need not brag
Impassive planets are more fortunate.
Has the man ever lived who from his birth
Was not love's bleeding prey? A mourning dove
First moaning for his nurse, then for his mate?
Or else a cuckoo, mocking as he's mocked?
Frustration and despair are most men's fate,
Beating on doors that are forever locked
Some leaping down from the Leucadian crag.
And yet there *is* a way – it's Dante Alighieri's
Who called the god of love by his real name
The name carved on the Cross by Pontius Pilate,
The name invoked with sobs by the two Marys
The day they sought Him in the empty tomb!
Each one of us abides love's doom.
They talk of 'crossed in love', yes *Crossed*,

By love our souls are saved, by love our souls are lost.
The code of courtly love is that of Christ:
To take rebuffs and not resent the shame;
To bide with cheerfulness the broken tryst;
To welcome joys in which we have no part;
To laugh to scorn self-pity's grumble;
Always to choose the better part.
To do these things demands humility,
The only balsam for the inward smart
And which the God of Love said 'Learn of Me...'
Was ever anyone by *nature* humble?

Love Lies Dying

'Love lies bleeding' is the old song
Or is it from the Greek Anthology?
At any rate the god is Cupid
Whose soft little foot is wounded by a thorn.
But when it is the great and terrible god of love
Who received Dante into his discipline
And led him to salvation
Who lies dying – no other deathbed is as terrible as this,
Because the meaning of one's life dies with him
And our god-spun destiny is betrayed.
Great God! Save me from a love that dies.

To Mrs Patrick Campbell
(With the Plays of Euripides,
after having seen her as Electra)

The gracious form of Greece died long ago,
That form, elusive, godlike, golden, white,
Its fragrant ashes scattered by the winds
Of stormy Time. And yet no soul can die.
And so the Soul of Greece, immortal springs
From places strange, when men least look for her.
Radiant, triumphant, glorified by sleep,
She whispers in each lyric poet's song,
She twines herself around our secret dreams,
And Beauty ever hides her in her heart.
But yet, 'tis hard to see the formless soul,
And I in blindness, had long wept her dead,
Until one day I knew her face in you,
She strangely smiled thro' your Electra's tears.
And then I knew that she had gained thro' woe,
And on her whiteness purple flowers had bloomed
Of grief, despair, and agonies of love.
Of pangs of mystic child-birth, and of hate.
And so if Sophocles from dazzling heights
Of cold Olympus, 'mong his changeless gods,
Had gazed with wise child-eyes upon her now,
This strange bright blossom of the Grecian Soul,
He would have turned in nameless dread and awe
To hide within the flawless, virgin arms
Of his Antigone, dreading strange gods.
But yet, that other, with his subtle smile,
With soul as strange and fierce as this new Greece,
Euripides – sober, yet vine crowned, bitter-sweet –
Would hail this flame-like Greece, new born in you,
As that which he had known in secret dreams.

To Jean, Who Loves Faerie-tales

When people are small with curly hair
And rosy and not *too* fat –
Then they can do the most lovely things
As squeezing themselves down rabbit holes
And play with Alice in Wonderland.
And because they are small the other small things
Squirrels and dogs and birds
Will not be afraid as with grown ups
But will play with them in the summer-woods
And tell them their secret too.
And when they are tucked in their comfy beds
And hot and rosy with sleep –
The Lady of Dreams who loves the dream-child
Will take them on her knee
And tell them stories that never end
Of spirits and children and flowers –
And tucks them safely back in bed
And kisses them on the hair –
And then flies back to her wonderful house on the morning's rosy
                                                                                     wings.

And *sometimes* when they have been *very* good
The Faeries lead them away –
To where their yellow-skirts whisk in the moon
And there are other children there and a few grown-ups as well
Who have been given the freedom of Elfin town and can never
                                                                                        really grow old.

Thomas the Rhymer and I think Charles Lamb
And Shakespeare, Kilmeny and Keats
And many whose names we don't know as well
Whose hearts are light though their hair is gray
And their eyes are glad though their brows are lined.
And perhaps some day when you're grown up
If you are gentle and kind
And love all the children with all your might
And most if they are hungry and cold
And feed the sparrows with lots of crumbs
And never say Faeries aren't true
And read lots and lots of faerie books

Then perhaps this will come to you
They will make you a member of Elfin-Town
And then if people are ever unkind
Or Life is sad and dull
You won't mind a bit, though your body is tired
For you are one that understands
And your soul is miles and miles away
Dancing glad with the Faerie-Folk.

The Moon-Flowers

The moon-flowers white
Are here, maddening the fervent summer night
With their hot scent that yearns like a strange sigh,
Wherein is hid the secret pale and sad
That haunts the moon, her dreams that turn men mad,
Her love, her silver songs that draw the sea;
As all the music of the nightingale
Is found within the scent of one red rose.
'Tis you, not Lilies, should have graced the pale
Wan maid Elaine, moon-like in haunting love –
And well I ween, that the Greek shepherd lad
Who madly sought your Queen through Arcady
Entwined you in his hair,
While in his ear strange messages of love
You whispered from his *Laydie* pale above
And sad Ophelia should have wound you with her rue
And rosemary – remembrance, and despair,
For you would bring forgetfulness and night.
Yes, when we feel your scent all is forgot
Save that life is a blossom strange and white
Intoxicating, cruel, fervent, and hot,
Which we must pluck. – And then before our sight –
It fades and dies as swiftly as do you.

Love

Maids dream of Love to be a mighty King,
As did the Jews of their Messiah
Coming with sword of fire,
Clad in brave garments and with purple wing
To storm their hearts and reign there supreme.
Ah! Rosy maiden dream!
There is no minstrelsy
To herald him. He comes meek-browed, alone,
And creeps into their hearts. And ere he's known,
Their Love they crucify.

And golden youths swear in their pride to give
Their life, their warm limbs and their keen, white sword
In services to this Lord
This Love, the greatest of all gods that live.
They wander till the years have left them old,
As is the legend told
Of Christopher the Saint, seeking their god.
And Lo! He comes, a child with wistful eyes,
But in their arms heavy as Lead he lies
To bear across the flood.
And old folk weep o'er Love as long since dead,
And think with yearning of its hair's lost gold,
Its warm flesh now grown cold
Ah! Their dear Love had lips so sweet, so red,
That know no kisses now but Death's, alas!
Why must all sweet things pass?
And yet Love all the day
Sits by them, tends them well, nor do they guess
That Love is with them in their loneliness,
Gray Love, grown old as they.

Carpe Diem

Oh! May I make each moment of my life a gem,
Flawless and brilliant, blazing with white flame,
Glowing with red, burning with blue, yet all the same
In brilliance. So in old age when I look back on them
Their blaze combined may turn life to a diadem.

Or may I turn each moment to a flower,
Those of seclusion violets, mistry, rare,
Moments of passion roses, lilies for those of prayer,
That when I come to my last fading poppied hour
On looking back my fragrant life may seem a bower.

Or may each moment be a dream of rare
and gorgeous dyes – some green as peacocks' wings,
Some pink and amethyst like twilight things,
All woven by some unseen loom up there
Into the starry robe my deathless soul shall wear.

My Soul Was a Princess

My soul was a princess who dwelt in state
In a palace vast and white as the moon,
All of silver and pearls seemed her wan, proud fate,
Her day was dawn with no hope of noon.
Like shrouds were her garments of violet silk,
Her sleeves were strange sad dreams half-born,
Her face was wan, and her skin like milk,
Her eyes were gray, chill, yearning as dawn.
And she sat and wept 'mong her blossoms white,
Sad blooms, like the ghosts of long dead woes
Till her hair brushed earth like a pinion of night,
And she cried: 'All my kingdom for one red rose!'

The Moon-Maid

A Moon-Maid sat in her garden of dreams
'Mid the pale gold flowers of her mind
And dreamed of the love that she would find
Hid in her garden some dim, strange day,
Many moon-days away –
Gold wings hid 'mong golden flowers
White limbs hid 'mong snow white hours,
And crimson lute
Hid 'mong the purple fruit.
And her voice plained forth like faerie streams:
'Oh! perchance in a mist of golden rain
As it came to maids of old
Will it come some day to me
And melt my form in eternity,
'Till nought but the flames of my soul remain
To burn rose-red thro' the gold.
Will it come with Elfin storms and strife
Or dream in a fair green field
Filled with unearthly, starry, Grecian peace
Where wayward maiden thoughts must cease,
Where culls Hippolytus the mystic charms
That teach him all the cold white things of god?
Will it be a man with a woman's hair
And wild sad eyes wherein is sealed
The curse that comes from knowledge of vast things?
Or a Titian maid gigantic, still
Like her once sung by Baudelaire?
Or a child that was reared by Faerie hands
Still hot and rosy from Elfin sleep
And wise with the wisdom the wise stars keep?
Or a calm Caryatid might bloom into life
And let me lie in her great white arms,
While I kissed the head that had born the abode
Made for a god by a hero's hands. . .'
The Moon-Maid ceased, within her moth-like eyes
The dream-flowers closed like buds at Even-song;
The world crept slowly into that strange tower of sighs
And songs that was her mind,
As the blue shadow of a great bat's wings

Falls on the pretty, dancing faerie-folk;
The leaves were rustled by a human foot –
It was a man. No clinging mysteries
Cast round him as aroma of unearthly things
Unless the secrets that one learns from Earth,
And gentle, wistful, half-born dreams, that throng
Round weary simple folk beside the goblin fire.
His eyes were not a god's: but wondrous kind,
And very gentle in their pure desire.
He gazed on her a while, and then he spoke:
'Oh! Little Moon-Maid come with me to Earth,
For it is warm as this cruel moon is cold,
I have a home for thee'. She dropped her amber lute,
The dream-flowers died within her wondering eyes,
And in them, haply, something else had birth –
The only human thing that ne'er grows old.

from My Mother's Pedigree

My mother's pedigree
Is the first symphony
Of Mahler

Birds sing at its beginning and its end – but they
Are curlews singing over lonely cairns.
And the two keys clash and fight with
Battle axes and claymores, and all is blood
And tears and the flowers of the forest
That will never bloom again and little princess
Matilda hugging her belly to shelter what
Is in it and to hide it from the Bruce's
Awful eyes, storming at her in Norman-French
And the Black Knight of Lorn who is so
Debonair and her great grandson and her Jewish
Lover. And all through rung sweet thin
Pastoral music – the meagre beauty of West Lothian
That embattles Dundas of Dundas
Laverils that sing no leafy song
But in the faint-blue sky, the gardens where

Gooseberries and single roses grow and everything has
A delicate meagreness the   of a thin poor soil
And the shattering beauty of Strathearn and Lorn and
Atholl. Earl Beardie, Rizzio, the fierce
Ogilvies. And yet all of it by the tectonics of
A thousand genes builds – me, who am at
Least articulate.

The Faerie Changelings

From the vales of the moon, from the woods of the sea,
    The Faerie Changelings come,
  And the dreams of the moon lie deep in their eyes,
  And their smile is strange with sea mysteries,
  Yet oh! they can laugh right merrily,
    But woe to their earthly home!

For their tongues are cruel, tho' their lips are sweet,
    And they know not love nor hate
  And a viper lurks 'neath their flower-like ways,
  Nor know they the menace of passing days,
  Nor of stones and thorns beneath their feet,
    Nor of joy that comes too late.

For tho' their bodies to earth are bound;
    By the laws of penance dire
  For snake-like elfin sins, they love in Hell
  The sins of dim strange dreams, that none dare tell,
  Yet their souls can pass beyond mortal sound
    Thro' the Elfin gates of fire.

Around them on earth, cities rise and fall;
    And their earthly loves may die,
  Or writhe and shriek thro' their hearts' despair,
  And men may be fierce or loving or fair –
  And the ghost of love in the wind may call,
    Still they smile mysteriously.

> For their souls hold revel in Faerie-land,
>   And they see what they dare not tell,
>   And their ears hear tunes that would turn men mad,
>   And their hearts are cruel but oh! so glad,
>   For they know a joy that by God is banned –
>   For they fear not book nor bell.
>
> And the Furies lead to their arms so white,
>   The men that they wish to beguile,
>   And the form they embrace turns into a snake,
> [. . .]

'Some talk of Alexander and some sing Monty's praise'

Some talk of Alexander and some sing Monty's praise,
Churchill was the world's hero in Britain's finest days;
Some think a lot of Stalin and Marshal Tito, too,
The Frogs admire their dear de Gaulle, (though English seldom do!)
And each one backs his fancy, each thinks his favourite's best,
I[n] times of blood and toil and sweat and battle's awful test,
But Mappie says that Laurie Steele and also Charlie R,
Two very gallant ladies, have *really* won the war.

>   *Chorus*

Left! Right! Eyes front, look at the ladies now!
Lips compressed, neatly dressed, several medals upon each breast,
A red X upon each brow.
Takin' themselves very seriously, lookin' more grim than gay,
Hail! Laurie S and Charlie R. – the heroines of V DAY.

Churchill hides in his corner, Stalin sulks in disgrace,
Montgomery wears his beret now over his crestfallen face,
And Alexander is not at home (some say he's goin' to live in Rome)
'Ah! Perfide Albion', cries de Gaulle. For Charlie has usurped his role,
While Laurie wears the Victor's crown, these gallant ladies have done him down.

Poor Tito trembles in Bucharest, while Roosefeld sobs on Elinor's breast
And all male prestige is utterly gone, and Charlie and Laurie keep marchin' on!

(Repeat Chorus)

A Friendship

Delightedly, each, turning to the other
Plunges into strange waters, deep and sea cold
Echo of what is known. Here a shell,
A pebble, a strand of weed lies in the hand.
A counterpart, yet alien, glossed with foreign
Light, and all that lies beyond, in shadow,
Dark sea and promise. Now, like porpoises
Rolling over and moving through the water
They have become the dark brown shapes of laughter
Giving new brightness to a tired sea.

The Shooting Stars

After the long summer, languid with sun,
The dark sky, dusty with stars, cold, glittering, silent
Brought peace like sleep.

Then from the garden you saw the first star falling
And called me. 'Look,' you said. I was too late
For light's white leap.
But then standing together, both together
We saw the next star with a fang of ice
Furrow the night.

Perhaps this was foretelling, hard, star-pointed,
Our fortunes will scar the darkness of the future
In lines of light.

Ostia Antica

Now fountains play no more.
No wheel, no footfall, only
Cicada or swallow chattering.
The town lies bare and lonely.

Yet the warm skin of the sun
Smoothes the white marble's bone.
The lizard is a beating vein
Of life on the hot stone.
And the trembling butterflies
One after one drop down
To the turf crammed with its flowers,
And pavements notched with stone.

Stranded by time and the sea
Its roofless houses stand
Picked bare by the white sunlight
Like dry shells glittering on sand.
And yet quietly, with pity
The butterflies drop down,
Psyche and love to their dwelling.
The sun's blood warms the stone.

The Toad

On the black ridge of the road
Dank yellow oozed a toad.
The rain wet, steaming wood
Stretched, his ultimate good.
But simple, primaeval, he
Bulked there, content to be.

And we, whose thoughts outrace
Our wheels and our own pace
Stopped, seeing that clot of yellow
Whose life to ours was fellow.
A knop of being, whose cold
Skin throbbed with the heart it held.

The slow peace of the wood,
The drip of the rain like blood,
All this for a moment became
Our life, as too, for him,
Nothing beyond the breath.
Life springing from the fungus death.

Taking him in our hand
We lifted him beyond
The black ridge of the road.
And then we knew, the toad
Was compassion, the weight we hold,
Warm heart in a rind of cold.

The Invocation

by Anna de Noailles

Heart's city – listen while I sing to you – 'tis night,
    I come with heavy arms that all the world's love hold
    And poets, long since dead, down in their graves so cold
    Pursue me with desires, and know that *I* now live.

I am Time's sister; and the song that never dies;
    That shrill and burning cry, that makes the deep woods ring
    The adoration of the plants for Spring;
    Man's god-like haughty longing for the skies.

I am that fierce, impetuous endeavour,
    Despairing ever, and yet ever growing.
    The blood-stained awful face of madness knowing,
    That thinks it seeks for love, death wishing ever.

I am that which all makes drunk, and yet all grieves,
　　Whose heart beats oft so loud, and feels so great,
　　That Samson lifting Gaza's mighty gate,
　　Seems to have plucked a lily and its leaves.

Listen heart's city – 'tis I am your Salambô,
　　Who stands upon the terraces in a mist of gold,
　　What time in space in langorous rings unfold
　　Desire's fair form and wings – splendid in woe.

The wisdom of the ages dreams 'neath my soul's flight,
　　A sword, like to a lily with a thorn, pricks deep
　　Into my heart. I lift my arms unto the skies that weep,
　　Romantic Pallas of the starry night!

I look – I listen, but my ears seem scarce awake,
　　For the sounds make nought but silence – silence which stills
　　All earth. The mighty silent cadence my blood fills
　　As with the sumptuous waves of an Italian lake.

A mesh of fair green silk my memory seems,
　　Where soft frail butterflies grow drunk with scent,
　　Where with the weight of bees the apple-trees are bent,
　　Where one by one the days long dead return like dreams.

In this mesh of my heart where the Kosmos is caught
　　Memory beckons and waves like a frenzied hand,
　　And the sycamore's leaves by the wind are fanned,
　　And the orange tree's scent flies swift as a thought.

Go! I can house you no longer within my heart,
　　Spirits of hot regrets and dreams. Become again
　　The spirits of the fire, the woods, the rain
　　Depart from out my life – I bid you all depart.

Become again the garden, or the cloud on high,
　　The scented roof of green upon the lemon tree,
　　The rose-bush prouder than the perfumed faerie sea,
　　The frankness of the bird, or of the morning sky.

Let dust and ashes turn to dust again,
    And let my childhood be my childhood, nothing more,
    Instead of that great load of all I did adore,
    And which my fingers strive to seize in vain.

And let the dead stay dead, and be no longer prest
    As shadows to my heart, the while I murmur low –
    'You are my dreams, my storms, my woe.'
    And let me clutch no longer tombs unto my breast.

And then, set free of this my heart's fierce burn,
    Bearing no more the world attached to me,
    At last, I may repose beneath a great, calm tree,
    And with some pure fresh water fill my urn.

And having hurled from off my heart this stone,
    Ah! that once more beneath the hawthorn tree,
    I may be like a maid, dreamy and fancy free,
    Who thrills with hope towards a love unknown.

Dusk

by Albert Samain

The Angel of Dusk glides over the flowers. . .
The Lady of Dreams sings at Evensong;
The skies where day grows fair with gold prolong
The gorgeous death-pangs of the waning hours.

The Angel of Dusk fans our hearts with his wings. . .
And maids from the breezes love odours inhale,
While o'er the flowers and o'er the maidens frail
There falls the Lovely dimness of dream-things.

The garden roses droop with weary grace
And Schumann's soul adrift in silent space
Seems to tell of a never dying woe. . . .

Somewhere surely a wan child life dies slow.
Oh! My soul put a mark in the book of years,
The Angel will gather this dream from your tears.

ESSAYS

Some Aspects of the Art of Alexey Mikhailovich Remizov

Alexey Mikhailovich Remizov is considered by many Russians to be their greatest living writer. I cannot here deal with all the sides of his genius; for it has many sides – there is a Gogol side, a Dostoevsky one, and, like most of his Russian contemporaries, he is not a little influenced by the demonology of Madame Blavatsky. Then, there is an element of Caliban in him, and an element of Ariel – an element, too, of St Francis of Assisi, though he never *preaches* to birds and elements, or, indeed, to anybody.

He is, on the whole, an optimist; but it is a curious optimism, part mystical, part whimsical, not unlike that expressed in the song from *Pippa Passes*:

> The snail's on the thorn,
> God's in his heaven,
> All's right with the world!

Browning, however, as even his most ardent admirers will admit, writes with an accent, and in Pippa's song the accent is very strong. But eliminate the accent, substitute a sly tone for a hearty one, let there be, by all means, a tear in *one* eye – so long as there is a twinkle in the other; while the ghost of a wink draws the attention to the new Table of Precedence, which ordains that a snail shall 'go in' before God – and you have the quiddity of a certain aspect of Remizov. It is the optimism of a humorist; and it is as a humorous writer that Alexey Mikhailovich is most successful.

The power of physical identification with the things one is writing about is one of the attributes of the comic genius as opposed to the tragic. Rabelais when he is writing about Gargantua certainly feels like a giant himself; and we are convinced that the body of Swift swells or contracts according to whether Gulliver is at that moment in Brobdingnag or Lilliput. But on to the white sheet of Melpomene the tragedian projects the conflicts of *his own* soul – and it is just for that reason that they are tragic; for about one's neighbour and his experiences there is always something just a little comic. One has only to read the description in the second part of *On a Field Azure* of the fussy, busy, old house-dog Kushka to realize that Alexey Mikhailovich possesses in a high degree this power of physical identification. When he looks at a dog, he begins to feel the fleas biting; when he looks at the Petersburg pavement in August, he feels thirsty; and then he sets to to write about them – the dog and the pavement – with exquisite imaginative humour. But his power of identification is not merely physical. When, for instance, he writes about a child, it is not only that his legs become a little wobbly, and that the ox-eyed daisies are tickling his chin, but, as well, he 'speaks as a child, understands as a child, thinks as a child.' And it is this power of psychical as well as physical identification that gives to his humour the tenderness and profundity of Lamb – that fine sense of the exact 'values' in the light and shade of moral phenomena that is the final grace of the intellect.

We have said that in Alexey Mikhailovich there is something of both Caliban and Ariel – but a Caliban and Ariel who have held in their hands, throbbing like a bird, the secret heart of Miranda. Olga, the heroine of *On a Field Azure* is own sister to Pushkin's Tatiana and Tolstoy's immortal Natasha – and what higher mead of praise is there than this? Olga's first lover is a student who has been tutor to her brother during the summer holidays. When he gets back to Moscow he writes her long tender letters all about his hopes and ambitions and dreams,

> Olga wrote him in answer one or two very short little notes. For one thing, she wasn't fond of writing letters, and besides each of his gave her a curious feeling (and the tenderer the letter, the stronger was this feeling) – it was a feeling of oppression, arising from the fact that he had a right to write to her in that way, and to be hoping for and expecting something from her. And the feeling of oppression would turn into irritation, to hatred of him.

There is no need to comment on the almost uncanny penetration of this analysis. Writers are too apt to forget, these days, that in many young girls there is still left an element of the Nymph.

Alexey Mikhailovich has another faculty, which, as in the case of his great master, Gogol, blends oddly with his humour – that of *exaltation*: the *exaltation* that has been so penetratingly analyzed by Monsieur Charles du Bos in his beautiful essay on Proust. This *Exaltation*, says Monsieur du Bos, is the source of all forms of spiritual activity, and comes to be so closely identified with the sense of life itself that, at the moment we are experiencing it, everything beyond its zone seems stricken by death. It is the 'éther sur lequel nous sommes portés, elle est, non le message distinct, mais l'onde qui transmettra tous les messages possibles, ou, si l'on préfère, l'enveloppe, l'impalpable tunique protectrice qui rend invulnérable, glorieux, le corps de toute vérité prête à surgir.' And he applies to it Joubert's words on Plato's style: 'Il y a en lui plus de lumière que d'objets, plus de formes que de matière.'

And, to use a more material metaphor which I am sure Monsieur du Bos will pardon, that which is written under its influence has more bouquet than body.

It is, in fact, the intermittent power of seeing phenomena in a magnifying and golden atmosphere – an atmosphere that acts on the vocal chords as well as on the optic nerve; and when the voice continues trembling after the golden light has faded, then sentimentality is born. But Alexey Mikhailovich is never sentimental – as soon as the glory has departed his voice resumes its habitual tones of sly humour.

The exact meaning of words written under the influence of *exaltation* does not bear too close a scrutiny. What, for instance, is the exact meaning of the little refrain, *Fate, Bride, Spring*, that haunts the second part of *On a Field Azure*? All it means is that, for the moment, the life of this little Russian girl is caught up to that other plane, which, in the words of Monsieur du Bos, is 'antérieure à ceux qui tombent sous la catégorie de notre connaissance.' One of the characteristics of *exaltation* is that it is transmittable, and, at these moments, Olga has for us too something unearthly about her; or, rather, in that she is at once radiant and familiar, she has, like the lovely girls of Tennyson, (the Gardener's Daughter, Olivia of the Talking Oak), some of the glamour of those creatures who cannot breathe out of their native element – the memory: our parents' memory, for that always seems a more golden element, inhabited by more radiant creatures, than our own; and like that same Olivia and Gardener's Daughter, she stands in a picture by Monet, static, and smiling, and flecked with leaf-filtered sunshine.

The Teapot, too (one of Remizov's most famous short stories), is woven from this mixture of humour and *exaltation*. During the early days of the War, Gerasimovich, a minor civil servant, stays on grilling in Petersburg through August, bound to his stuffy noisy flat by the pseudo-patriotic obligations of reading the daily papers, and following the movements of the troops with little flag-topped pins on his great map of the front. 'And yet he was told that the meadows had never been so full of flowers as during that cruel fatal summer, dulled though its radiance was by grief and blood; and in Moscow the limes had such marvellous blossom – all Moscow was in flower.

The suburbs were full of bees, not knowing where to fly. In the Kremlin a swarm had actually settled on the tower of Ivan the Great.' Finally, however, he yields to the persuasions of a friend to come and stay with him in his remote country house, and intoxicated by the thought of greenness and fragrance and, above all, of quiet, he sets off. But, alas! he finds the house crammed from garret to cellar with refugees! That in itself is sufficient to shatter his dream of peace, but, in addition, a room has been prepared for him in a cottage in the grounds which his host had given to a Polish refugee, Pani Maria. Pani Maria is to 'do' for him. There is but a thin wooden partition between his room and the Pani's, and her baby yells all night. And, what is much worse, Pani Maria is one of these people whose lips are tight and bosom heaving with suppressed grievances, and she makes Gerasimovich feel a heartless brute every time he asks her for some shaving-water or a cup of tea. Finally, the emotional climax is reached when Gerasimovich breaks a teapot of the Pani's; for her silence becomes so ominous, her outraged feelings so oppressive, that he flies in terror back to Petersburg.

This, in spite of the sensitive, exquisite, nature of the hero, is comedy. Man is fundamentally a Stoic, (he would never have survived if he had not been), and this Stoicism forbids him to treat the minor discomforts of life, and such phenomena as that of a trifle, taking on vast dimensions for exacerbated nerves, in anything but a comic vein. This is one of the unwritten canons of literature. It would be interesting to trace the psychological origins of these canons – they are the secret arbiters of literary *genres*. Now and then they are broken, but, as a rule, it is better to observe them, and *The Teapot* is written in the lightest most whimsical of styles – except when the sweetness of life's sorrows and joys becomes too great for Alexey Mikhailovich and, like the bees on the Kremlin, his page swarms. All through this little story the great plain of Russia is blossoming, a million nightingales are serenading the same moon, and 'Rachel is weeping for her children and will not be comforted.'

But Alexey Mikhailovich is, perhaps, best known as a writer of legends, half fairy, half apocryphal, in which he catches to a marvel the rhythm and intonation of the speech of old Russia – old Russia, merry and pious, naïve and wise, sitting there immovable and turning the centuries with their tale of weal or woe, as they come surging up to break there at her feet, into little songs of fair Tsarinas, and golden birds that talk, and angels disguised as pilgrims. These stories of Alexey Mikhailovich are nearly all of them lovely, and some of them, as for instance the story of Christ, St. Nicholas, and the grey wolf, show the fundamental mysteries of the Christian faith in so delicate and tender a light as almost to vindicate the ways of God to man. Nevertheless, when one considers the almost irresistible claims of reality and the present upon every writer, one cannot help wondering what instinct, what *need* it is that drives Alexey Mikhailovich to write these stories. Some writers, it is true, crave for decorativeness – a curious craving in a writer and smacking more of a painter; because the majority of writers have no wish to tamper with life and the laws that govern it, but, springing aside to let the great thing roll past unimpeded (exhibiting, at the same time, a wise solicitude for their own skins), they watch, fascinated, the laws of dynamics and physics in ruthless and magnificent play. But for the decorative writers life is plastic and docile and malleable. If they choose, like William Morris they will place 'two red roses across the moon,' then stand back, head on one side, eyeing them critically. For what is life to them but a collection of beautiful objects: the lute, the orange, the printed page in strong black type, that the painter combines and readjusts according to his plastic needs? Life for the decorative writer is still-life. This tendency, when subjected to a rigid eclecticism – no object being admitted that is not strictly modern – will result in what for lack of a better name we will call *rococo* writing – the books wherein the writer's contemporaries and all their appurtenances are shown as small, grimacing, and amusing. Such, for example, are Pope's *Rape Of The Lock*, and, *parva componere magnis*, some of the stories of Oscar Wilde, *The Portrait of Dorian Gray* and *Lord Arthur Saville's Crime*.

But Alexey Mikhailovich is too humane to give free rein to this tendency; *Bojiy sviet* – 'God's world' is too solemn a place to be treated in this charming but frivolous manner. But man's world – the fantastic world built out of dreams and tradition – he is at liberty to treat as he chooses, and, ignoring the injunctions of Horace, to put a man's head on a horse's neck, and make a lady end in a fish's tail.

Behind these stories there is, perhaps, more of the antiquary than the decorator; and the true antiquary is an *amateur* of the Present rather than of the Past, for it is not dead things but dying ones that are the objects of his quest. Treading in the august footprints of Sir Walter Scott, he tracks an old tune to a shepherd whistling it in the hidden valley where it was born, chases winged words with his net, listens to old wives' tales, and hastens to catch the last faltered words of the dying gods. And it must be remembered that the material of Alexey Mikhailovich's legends – the language in which they are written, the attitude to life that they express – though on the brink of labefaction, is still alive. The lesson learned by the antiquary is how 'quick bright things come to confusion,' and that the Present too is perishable, for, being born of the Past, it carries in it the fatal seeds of its parentage, and must inevitably, in its turn, itself become the Past. From this wistful attitude to the present, as a thing foredoomed before its birth, it is an easy step to the delusion that it *is* the past and, hence, static and solid – a thing that one can turn round in one's hand and examine at one's leisure, dwelling lovingly on its details; and most of Alexey Mikhailovich's modern stories read as if they were reconstructions of the past. He treats the present with the reverend accuracy of the antiquary, handling it delicately and lovingly, as if it were a rare and very fragile object; and this is not the same as treating it merely decoratively – 'the learned eye is still the loving one.'

This is one of the sources of Alexey Mikhailovich's full and brimming page. It is surely not merely a delusion of the present writer's that the pages of some writers – and they often among the greatest – are, if isolated from the cumulative effect of the whole book, thin and unsatisfying to both the ear *and the eye*. We all know the sense of almost physical discomfort that comes on us when we pass in the train a poor soil, sparsely sown with meagre crops – and then the joy, a few miles further on, with which the eye gluts itself on a full brimming field of ripe tawny wheat. A similar impression is experienced on turning from the pages – taken as separate entities – of Tolstoy and George Eliot to those of such writers as Alexey Mikhailovich. Tolstoy and George Eliot are soldiers under marching orders – though I doubt if they know who is their captain or what their bourne. But it is not for them to linger by the way, picking the roadside flowers and watching the sunset. They may move as slowly as they like, but they must keep moving. But Alexey Mikhailovich is a free lance, and, together with his rich vocabulary, it is the little details, pretty and gratuitous like the *flora* and *fauna* round a medieval manuscript, that make his page full and brimming.

Nevertheless, the full and brimming page can be produced without a rich vocabulary or a pullulation of detail, as is proved by the fact that it is always to be found in the writings of these two highly economical artists – Jane Austen and Defoe. Defoe is primarily an observer. His art is static rather than dynamic; the action has already taken place, and does not grow under one's eye. Hence, from a certain stagnancy, it is easier for his pages to be full and brimming than for those writers whose pages are in flux. In all this he differs very much from Alexey Mikhailovich who is not really an observer, but a re-creator. Alexey Mikhailovich is obsessed by the desire to possess, by re-creation, every bright object that he sees. And while his attention is focused on it the bright object becomes the only thing that matters – for the time being it *is* the story. Jane Austen, however, differs from both Defoe and Alexey Mikhailovich in that she too is under marching orders and subject to the same invisible captain as Tolstoy and George Eliot; and part of the fascination of her books is due to the perennial pleasure we take in watching tiny things obeying those laws to which vast bodies are also subjected – it is like turning from the battles of Eneas and Turnus to those of the bee chieftains in the *Fourth Georgic*. But – and in this she resembles Defoe – she has a sharper eye, a more decided mind, than either Tolstoy or George Eliot, and is able to abstract to its essentials a character or a situation. One has only to read the few lines at the end of the second chapter of *Pride and Prejudice* with which she sums up the character of Mrs Bennet, and those in which Defoe makes Roxana sum up her married life, to realize that with these two writers every word tells. And, naturally, a page on which every word is valuable gives an impression of richness.

I should like to develop a little my view as to Alexey Mikhailovich's attitude to details; for it is essential to the understanding of his art. There is an English writer who, at first sight, must seem of all the writers in the world the most remote from him, but whose methods, however different may be his results, are not dissimilar – I mean Walter Savage Landor. What resemblance, you may well ask, can there possibly be between that whimsical, loveable, Russian child of nature, and this fierce, intolerant, old English Roman? Between the living, warm, wayward, tender style of the one, and the pure disoxygenized atmosphere of the other's quintessential English? It is just this, that for Landor always, and for Alexey Mikhailovich often, their books are the depository of their collection – the small blue and white and freckled eggs that they so gleefully rifle from the visible world; while the writing of them is a sort of game. This is Landor's game: he has to fit into or adapt to the conditions and circumstances of the characters in his dialogues as many as possible of the amusing, or pretty, or recondite facts that he has collected from his observation of the present, or his reading about the past; as many as possible, also, of the epigrams and elegant phrases that have come into his head without a context. And when we read Landor we have continually the impression of the head of an ox-eyed daisy being adroitly severed from its stalk by the swishing cane of a pedestrian, who is still enough of the boy to lighten his walk through the fields by this innocent amusement. This impression of a collection and a game is certainly not so strong, or so constant, in reading Alexey Mikhailovich. For one thing, as we have seen, he is prone to 'exaltation' – and when we are in that condition we cease to play. But one has only to read what is perhaps his masterpiece, the story called *Ivan Semenovich Stratilatov*, to be convinced that, firstly, the present is here a thing completely static and solid, and secondly, that it is made of a fabric woven out of a myriad separate brightly coloured little threads to the collecting of which Alexey Mikhailovich has brought the gusto of an amateur, in the weaving together of which he has found the amusement of a game. And if one turns to the pages of *Madame Bovary*, full and brimming though they be, one feels the difference. Take almost any page you like, the page that describes Emma's walk with Léon to the cottage where her baby is out at nurse; the pages that describe the *Comices*, or Emma's first ride with Rodolphe – and you will find none of the solemn marching forward of George Eliot and Tolstoy, and such a wealth of detail that it seems as if Flaubert had squandered on each page the whole store of his observations. But this is no game – Flaubert is always in deadly earnest, he has no time and no inclination to make a collection of facts and details for their own sake, and then combine them into a pattern; for him they are but tools to help him in his gigantic task of reconstructing, stone by stone, the visible universe out of words.

The adjective 'Russian' is frequently applied to Remizov by his compatriots; as it is also to Pushkin and Gogol, though never to Tolstoy or Dostoevsky. The Russians cannot define what they mean by the adjective in this sense, and one suspects behind their use of it a subconscious but important classification. A particular use of 'Shakespearian' that I have recently observed may perhaps help us to understand what it is exactly that they mean. Recently our most exquisite living writer made a speech at a literary dinner, and one of the guests described it as 'Shakespearian': 'I don't mean that she made the sort of speech that Will Shakespeare *himself* would have made, but it was like something in a Shakespeare play', she added, showing by this explanation that the meaning of the word in this particular sense has not quite yet emerged from our national subconsciousness.

Like something in a Shakespeare play – like 'Tomorrow and tomorrow and tomorrow', or 'Put out the light'? Surely not; for these great speeches are scarcely 'after-dinner speeches'. Besides, they have the unmistakable accents of Will Shakespeare's *own* voice – and to this, as the guest had shown herself aware, the adjective, in this sense, is never applied.

When the meaning of a word has not yet crystallized, it is on the lips of those that use it that we must study it. I have heard 'Shakespearian' applied to the gossip of old village women, to Herrick, to the 'Aunts' in *The Mill on the Floss*; and our greatest Shakespearian scholar, Mr Andrew Bradley, in a lecture on Jane Austen applied it to Mr Woodhouse. It is applied to 'characters', to the humours of old-fashioned provincial life, to a sort of sweet fooling, and to the strains of that shepherd's pipe that, though it may play different tunes, sounds through the life and traditions of every nation. Is, then, 'Shakespearian' a synonym of 'very English'? No, for I have never heard *Punch* called 'Shakespearian', nor the Book of the Common Prayer, nor the National Anthem. It is a particular aspect of English things – in fact, 'the still small voice' of England, which, we flatter ourselves, none but natives can hear. We, when we are in foreign lands, with our country so firm and safe behind us, can afford lovingly to mock at that little voice, and listen to it with a smile. Artegnan's béarnais accent made the Captains of the Musketeers smile, because it reminded him of his youth and his country – 'double souvenir', says Dumas, 'qui fait sourire l'homme à tous les âges.'

But for the Russians in exile? All Moscow is in flower, and everything is so sweet that the bees swarm on the tower of Ivan the Great.

When the Moscow Art Theatre was playing here last year, one realized that for the Russians it was now their native land – a troop of strolling players performing mimic actions as people who had never been.

For they who say such things declare plainly that they seek a country: these words of St Paul might serve as the motto to every text book on Russian history – a race of pilgrims wandering over a vast plain, founding and abandoning first one city and then another, Kiev, Moscow, Petersburg.

A great deal of sentimental nonsense has been written about the Russians; but the fact remains that they are the most spiritual-minded of all people. *For they who say such things declare plainly that they seek a country* – a house not made with hands, a land of ghosts and shadows. Perhaps it is only in exile that the Russians have found their home.

What an inadequate account this is of the writings of Alexey Mikhailovich! Sadly inadequate as touching both their matter and style, while the *tertium quid* has completely evaded my pen. But criticism is at best a thankless task, and reading is almost as hard an art as writing, especially if the books are by a sincere and talented writer; because he leaves so much unsaid. Every man and woman, worthy of the name, is an Initiate; but each is an Initiate into different Mysteries. Hence we walk among our fellows with the mysterious and slightly pitying smile of an adept among catechumens. And we have no need to take a vow of secrecy; because we are incapable of revealing what we know. But writers are garrulous, confiding creatures and would so willingly impart their own unique secret – in vain! They are like ghosts who, burdened with a message of tremendous import, can only trail their chains and gibber. Perhaps the measure of a writer's greatness is just the disparity between the things he says and the things he knows.

Listening in to the Past

'Have you seen the hat of the gardener's daughter?'
'No, but I have seen the pen of the excellent grocer's niece.'

Not only does this seem to me *per se* an excellent way of beginning an essay, but, as well, it provides me with a rhetorical model for expressing my own feelings: *Do you like listening in? No. But I am very fond of a kaleidoscope.* Indeed, it surprises me that this taste is not universal, for a kaleidoscope is the prettiest toy ever invented, and the most entertaining of all the thieves of time. It is a beautiful word, too, and sounds like the name of one of the Muses. However, I do not think the toy was known to the Greeks. If it had been, Plato would surely have founded upon it a cosmographical myth.

Do you like listening in? No, but I am haunted by the Past. A swift, fleeting sense of the past is as near as I have ever got to a mystical experience. . .a sudden *physical* conviction (like fingering for the first time the antiquity one had so often gazed at through the glass case in the museum), that Horace and Virgil did *really* once travel together to Brundusium, and that Horace was kept awake by mosquitoes and the love-songs of tipsy boatmen – Latin love-songs sung by Roman boatmen; or, that at a definite point of time the larks were singing and there were milestones on the Dover road, as Chaucer jogged on his way to Canterbury.

And now I come to the justification (in my case) of the famous Ollendorffian *But*. If the time ever comes when we can listen in to the past, I shall immediately order a wireless, though this will be due more to my love of a kaleidoscope than to my love of the past. My knowledge of the relation between sound-waves and etherwaves is of the vaguest, nor do I know anything about electricity, magnetism, or the Quantum Theory, nevertheless I am sure it will be very difficult to control the old fragments of human speech blown in from the waste places of the universe to be lost again for another thousand years. No, it will be an aural kaleidoscope, rather than a lesson in history: disparate fragments of Cockney, Egyptian, Babylonian, Provençal, ever forming into new patterns for the ear, but not for the mind. From time to time some immortal utterance may float past – Channing's voice booming out, 'We must defend Portugal', phrases from Pericles' funeral oration, the voice of the dying Goethe crying, 'Licht! mehr Licht!' Then the hoarse shriek of an English newspaper boy shouting last year's Derby winner, and trivial questions in some dead tongue: How many miles to Babylon? or, Where did you put my poisoned arrows? And the answer still a million miles away in space.

Yes, the written word, I fear, inadequate though it be, will never be superseded as the best means of telling us about the past. And here I must venture to disagree with that great humanist and historian, Mr George Trevelyan. He holds that Clio's best interpreter is literature; for instance, that it is in the Elizabethan plays that we get closest to the age of Elizabeth. But Literature, surely, is herself too great a Muse to take a back seat and let Clio do the talking. On the other hand, when it is the Law who tells us of old doings and old customs, there is nothing to distract our attention from her small dry voice.

The chief charm, to me, of certain Roman ruins – those at Trèves, for instance – consists in the fact that they are built of little bricks, and that wild flowers grow in their chinks. Bricks are, somehow, so much more intimate and homely than stones. And that other Roman fabric, the law, is built too of little bricks – homely details of everyday doings. So, when I want to listen in to the past, it is to old trials that I turn – to Pitcairn's 'Criminal Trials of Scotland', for instance. In Pitcairn the most amusing, in spite of the horror and cruelty of it all, are the witches' trials, for these it is that have most domestic details, so that we are continually getting whiffs of the homely acrid smell, like that of a peat-fire, of the Scotland of James VI.

It is comforting to learn that our ancestors were, on the whole, a little more credulous and naïve than we are. For instance, there was the cow-wife, Bessie Dunlop, whose familiar was the elf-bound ghost of a soldier killed at Pinkie. He seems to have been a benevolent and useful creature, as he helped her to discover stolen goods, and gave her herbs with which she cured gentle and simple of a 'cauld blood that came about their hearts', and of other mysterious sixteenth-century ailments. But he was not able to save poor Bessie from the stake.

Then there was Alison Pearson, who visited Elfland and danced at revels of the Fairy Queen, and was pinched and mishandled by the said Queen's mischievous subjects. There she saw 'auld Buccleugh' and Secretary Lethington 'that we belevit had been in heawin'. Let us hope that Secretary Lethington served the Queen of Fairie more faithfully than he had served the Queen of Scots.

Here, too, we shall find an account of the notorious Sabbath held at North Berwick by the leading witches and warlocks of Scotland.

They met at dead of night in a church, from the pulpit of which the devil wagged his black paw, and they each 'kissed his arse' and performed other ungodly rites that he might help them to raise a wind for wrecking the ship that was bringing the Queen from Norway.

But this was not the only sort of magic practised in Scotland in the sixteenth century. It was said of Mary Stuart that she exercised 'some enchantment, whereby men are bewitched', and the pages of Pitcairn that are the most vivid are those that concern, indirectly, this royal witch.

History, as a spectacle, is never so tragic nor so absorbing as when it shows us vast spiritual forces using as their tools the passions of individuals. And it is because of this that we feel an undying interest in the loves and hates of dead kings and queens.

The actors in the Queen Mary drama are only passionate puppets, but Titans pull the strings. It is not merely the schemes of Spain and the Vatican, the plots of Huguenot or Jesuit, that glint behind the dalliance of Mary and the amorous Chatelar, behind the quarrels and reconciliations with Darnley, behind the stormy scenes with Knox, behind, even (for Riccio, lord of the revels, was suspected of being an emissary from the Holy See) 'the wine and wax, the gaming and glee' of Holyrood. Nor is Elizabeth the most potent figure hidden behind the scenes – Elizabeth, with the vanity which served her for a heart, all pouts and blushes and excitement at the thought of the unknown girl cousin across the Border; poring over her portrait, which she keeps in the same casket as Leicester's, hoping that her hair is not as golden as her own, longing to possess her as a lovely, meek, adoring friend – and yet, politically, baulking her at every turn, never for a moment allowing her emotions to influence her actions. No, Elizabeth and the rest of them are, in their turn, but the tools of Destiny's monsters – the Reformation, the Counter-Reformation, the Birth of Modern Europe.

Mary was not like Elizabeth; she invariably followed her own inclinations. But, because of the peculiar circumstances of the time, these inclinations seemed always to chime in with the projects of one or other of the hidden powers. Then – as if conscious of this, as if determined once and for all to tear her life away from the loom of history – she gives her heart to James, Earl of Bothwell. Spain and France, Pope and Emperor may feel baffled and think their puppet has jerked itself free, but the monsters of Destiny smile grimly behind their masks. For Mary has never served their purpose better.

Well, all these matters are set out for our delight and instruction by Knox, and Buchanan, and Melville, and Brantôme in pages which, as one of her contemporaries said of Queen Mary's own style, 'want neither eloquence, despite, anger, love, nor passion.' But, after all, it is only with the pen that they tell their story. If we want to 'listen in', to hear the voices of the actors broadcast down the years, we must turn to the depositions of Bothwell's accomplices taken down verbatim and printed by Pitcairn among the 'Documents illustrative of the Murder of King Henry Darnley'. It may be fancy and due to nothing but the erratic spelling of the time, but in the deposition of 'French Paris' (the nickname given to a valet of Bothwell's whom he managed to get into the Queen's service shortly before the murder) we seem to hear the very *accent* of the prisoner. Bothwell becomes *Monsieur de Boduel*, John Hepburn *Jehan Hebron*, Glasgow *Glascou*, and so on. At any rate, we may amuse ourselves with the fancy that the clerk had his tongue in his cheek, and that our ancestors were as inordinately tickled as we are by French-English.

Poor 'Paris'! We cannot help feeling sorry for the time-serving, subtle rogue; for we know from his voice that his mouth is dry with terror. In vain does he pretend to have done his best to deter Bothwell from the deed, by invoking the holy name of *Monsieur le Comte de Morra*, the friend of the poor, the wisest, truest-hearted nobleman in Scotland (by whom he means Darnley's worst enemy, that cold-blooded schemer, the Regent Murray) – he was hanged, drawn, and quartered, and there is an entry in the Lord High Treasurer's accounts for that year of a few pence paid to a little boy for carrying his head and one of his legs to St. Andrews.

As for Bothwell himself, he stands out from these depositions as one of the most bloodthirsty ruffians who have ever lived. A terrible indictment against Bothwell and his circle is to be found in the confession of his kinsman and accomplice, the Laird of Ormiston, to his clergyman on the day of his execution. Ormiston made a most edifying end, certain of his own election, and confident that 'that night he would sup with God', in spite of having been, as he puts it himself, 'of all men on earth one of the proudest and heich myndit, and maist filthie of his body, abusing himself dyvers ways.' But for this he claims some slight excuse, seeing that 'within these seaven yearis bypast he never saw twa guid men, or ane guid deed.'

Nevertheless, we get the impression that Bothwell knew how to make love. From the deposition of 'French Paris' we learn that he sent the Queen a diamond, with the words, 'S'y j'avoy mon cuer je le luy envoyeraye, tres vollunties, mais je ne l'ay pas, moi.'

There is a particularly glorious kind of kaleidoscope for which you yourself provide the materials for the patterns. Under the lens there is a little tray, and on this you place any thin brightly coloured scraps you can lay hands on...the silver paper off chocolates, for instance, the petals of flowers, and so on. And, as you gradually add to this collection of scraps, you sometimes find – from the addition, say of a purplish-brown element given by a wallflower's petal or from the brilliant blue of a butterfly's wing, rifled from your childhood's collection – that both the colours and design of the patterns suddenly become much more beautiful. And (nor is this mere sentimentality, but it has, I feel convinced, a profound and philosophical explanation) the same thing will happen, when, into the kaleidoscope of sounds, with which we shall while away the winter evenings of the future, there float the words of some dead lover.

An Earthly Paradise

Fortunately for the weak and helpless there are many substitutes for the 'Friend behind phenomena' – good servants, for instance, kind aunts, a large balance at the bank. So if one is to realise adequately the horrors of the atheist's universe, it is necessary for a period to be cut off from these kindly sources of comfort...abroad, say, in a little unfriendly hotel, managed by people as impersonal as the *chauffage central*, and as cold; where everything, even a daily bath, is made as difficult as human, or, rather, as devilish ingenuity can compass, so that a few innocent cases of books make one feel as guilty and as helpless as a murderer seeking for a hiding-place for the remains of his victim; and whence one is driven daily, whatever the weather, to seek like Lear, as a witty friend most feelingly put it, one's omelette in the storm.

Such was our plight for a few miserable months in Paris till the kindest of friends removed us to a place where our ten trunks, five bonnet-boxes and three cases of books seemed mere pilgrim scrips, so monstrous, or, perhaps, I should say so *elephantine* were the trunks from across the Atlantic which that hospitable asylum housed by the score and the hundred; a place warm as only Americans know how to make their houses, where it was the custom to take at least two hot baths a day, and where the lady who looked after us was the best substitute for the 'Friend behind phenomena' that we are ever likely to have the good fortune to meet with. We felt like Casanova (though I trust we were more deserving!) when, his fortunes at their lowest ebb, he stumbles on a sort of Arabian Nights palace, founded by a pious and charitable lady for the entertainment of travellers, free of charge. For what with the state of the franc and the place being rent free, the charges were not beyond the means of the poorest scholars.

It was a fine old house in the *rue de Chevreuse*, and it had had an interesting history. It had originally been the private hotel of the Duchesse de Chevreuse (not the beautiful *Frondeuse* of whom Retz speaks in his memoirs, but her nineteenth-century successor) and there were still dark rumours afloat in the *quartier* of a daughter broken within these very walls on the wheel of the implacable matriarchy of the *Faubourg*. Then it became a boarding-house and entangled, how I have never quite understood, with the childhood of André Gide. Till he came to tea with us there, he had not been in it since he had grown up. It is the scene of certain of the episodes in his last and, many people think, his greatest novel, Les Faux Monnayeurs. Then it became an earthly Paradise for American girls studying art in Paris. During the war it was the American Red Cross hospital, and finally its owner, Mrs Whitelaw Reid, lent it to the American branch of the International Federation of University Women. To create is what makes life worth living; artists create books and pictures, philanthropists create happiness. In the memory of countless students – English and French as well as American – the image of Mrs Whitelaw Reid, like the statue of Dionysus in Alexandrian schoolrooms, will preside over the various lectures on abstruse subjects they attended at the Sorbonne, and such discoveries as may result from these studies they will offer I am sure, in their hearts, as a sort of votive offering to that kindly image. In spite of the sentimental belief to the contrary, a cheerless garret is not the best nursery for immortal works. The more comfortable one's body, the better one's mind is apt to function; and on this principal we had no excuse for idleness in the *rue de Chevreuse*... unless it were the best collection of fiction it has ever been my good fortune to browse in. As well as all the recent detective stories, our library contained many an extra-Barchester Trollope, which in England can only be read by the members of the London Library; nearly all the works of Charlotte M. Yonge and her followers – admirable books, which, while they give the French a depressing sense of the purity of our *mœurs*, are a perennial source of joy to all educated and humorous Englishwomen. The library contained, of course, many volumes that were not fiction, and the reason of our being so impressed by the number and variety of the novels was that it seemed a symbol of the whole spirit of the place, and of the gallant nation who had made it what it was – a nation that to a man and, what is still more striking, *to a woman*, have demanded from life, from the outset, cakes and ale as well as bread. And Life, if you make your demands with a pistol at her head, is apt to stand and deliver. The frequent ice-cream at dinner was another symbol of this attitude. Indeed, the food was delicious – a French groundwork, decorated by such exotic American dishes as Indian corn and strawberry shortcake – the frequent mention of which in the *Wide Wide World* and *What Katy Did*, have given so many of us a wistful longing to visit America.

Another entertaining characteristic of this most original of clubs was that one was apt to barge into André Maurois in the garden, or trip over Jules Romain in the corridor; the cause of this being that the French branch of the P.E.N. was allowed to hold its meetings in the club. Our club was in fact the centre of the communal life of the *quartier*, and it was a continual amusement to look down from the library on the ever-varying antics performed in the fine hall that was part of the annex built by Mrs Whitelaw Reid. Sometimes it was a company of douce Scots, laboriously learning the reel of Tulloch, the tune of which, as ground out on the piano by a patient, puzzled Frenchwoman, was no more the 'real Mackay' than are the fantastic *plèdes* the French imagine are tartans. Sometimes it was American children leaping round a Christmas tree. And one was even liable to catch a glimpse of the imposing mask-like face of Madame Curé, as she sat, weary and impassive, at some At Home given by a learned society.

The *rue de Chevreuse* runs between the *rue Notre Dame des Champs* and the *boulevard de Montparnasse,* and hence the club was so situated as to enable its members to make, if they chose, the best of both worlds. When provincials cast up their eyes over the wickedness of life in Paris, the Parisians smile, and ask them if they have ever walked down the *rue Notre Dame des Champs* at ten o'clock at night. And, indeed, Tartuffe himself could have found nothing to be shocked at by such an excursion. A grim, silent street it is. I doubt whether Aberdeen can be greyer or more puritanic, though I expect its architecture is not nearly as distinguished. The only colour in that street I ever remember to have seen were the reflections at night from the red and blue jars of the chemist's shop at the corner, as if fruits with coloured juices had been spilled over its grey asphalt surface. One was apt to see nuns in that street, on an average, say of two a week; and just as one begins to suspect by slow degrees that somewhere in one's garden is concealed a nest of insects, so in time we came to realise that the grim taciturn buildings that lined one side of the street were all of them contraband nunneries. Sometimes at their doors there would stop broughams which, to judge by the coronets emblazoned on their panels, and the extreme dowdiness of the ladies who emerged from them, came from the inner fastnesses of the *Faubourg Saint Germain*. But the *boulevard de Montparnasse* was a very different story; and actually a stone's throw from the club was the famous Rotonde, the café where Americans, Chinese, Swedes, Negroes – all nations in fact except the French themselves – congregate day after day to see what they fondly believe to be Life with a capital L. But Life, in spite of her capital, is a modest nymph, and apt to hide herself in unfrequented, obscure little crannies, where only those can enter who know the pass-word. What is the pass-word, and what is Life with a capital L? Perhaps as much as figment of the wistful romantic imagination of man as Fairyland or the Philosopher's Stone.

We, for our part, had no cravings after this nymph, and were quite content with the garden of the club. It was a very big one for a private house in a great city and possessed, in spring, the handsomest bed of wallflowers I have ever seen, and an acacia, and, even, a Judas tree. It was very amusing to watch the Judas tree at its tricks in the spring...first the unfolding of the funny nasturtium-like little leaves, and then the appearance of the tiny red blossoms, like the little Japanese sticks that one gets in very superior crackers, which unfold in water, under one's very eyes, into little paper flowers. And the back of an *immeuble* fronting another street served as an 'ivy mantled tower' to gaze at from one's bedroom window, for it was as thickly covered with ivy as any ruin of romance.

A little tin chapel was another of the ornaments of the garden – a humble vassal of the great American Episcopalian Church at the Etoile. On the principle of *suave mari*, it was very pleasant to sit of a Sunday morning in the arm-chairs of our comfortable study and listen to the strains of the *Te Deum* and of the *Church's One Foundation*, and, particularly, to the scrapings and shufflings of the congregation as they performed the exhausting gymnastics entailed by the ritual of the Anglican Church. We were fond of that little chapel. It was certainly far from decorative, but it seemed as friendly as the Judas tree, and as much a part of the garden; though, from its vocal powers it had, perhaps, more in common with the innumerable cats who regularly held their concerts there every night of the week. But strange rumours have reached us that the horn of the little chapel is to be exalted, and, from being but a humble denizen of the garden, it is to become the owner not only of the garden, but of the house, the hall, the endless bath-rooms – even, I suppose, of the complete works of Charlotte M. Yonge. It is like one of Pharaoh's dreams – the tiny animal that swells and swells till it swallows the whole herd. It seems to be our fate to pitch our tent on shifting sand – first the Paris club, then the Foundling property. At any rate, it stimulates our historical imagination and helps us to realise how such splendid, solid, conceptions as Babylon and Nineveh came to vanish from the face of the earth; or, rather, how the Vandals took possession of Rome. *Sic transit gloria mundi*.

The Religion of Women

A friend of mine has noticed that, if you catch them unawares, the faces of all middle-aged women are sad; the faces even of those whose circumstances have been uniformly prosperous. It is as if their bodies divined something that their minds ignored. Perhaps this is the mysterious *'phronema sarkos*, which some do expound the wisdom of the flesh' mentioned in the ninth Article of Religion. But sometimes this secret of the body flickers to the surface...when they are comfortable and off their guard, drinking tea with their cronies and chatting aimlessly. Suppose they have been discussing, though in no very profound or learned manner, the progress of modern science: how they remember hearing from their nurse, when they were little, of a prophecy of Mother Shipton that the day would come when men would fly, or how the telephone had been foreshadowed in the cartoon of an old *Punch*. And then, before you know where you are the atmosphere has suddenly become emotional. 'Yes', one of them murmurs dreamily, 'that's the way it goes!' And all of them have a tranced look in their eyes, and none of them is thinking of the progress of modern science – unless it can be looked upon as an aspect of what old Burton calls 'Ajax's time'.

> All things the long and countless years first draw from darkness, then bury from light.

Unwittingly they have given themselves away. The reason they look sad is that the ears of their body are always hearing the sound of: –

> Time's wingèd chariot hurrying near,

the chariot that leaves in its wake a cloud of dust, which is the past. And here the spirit comes in and takes a share of the sadness; for though it is the body that hears the chariot, it is the sprit that sees the dust. If, as Mrs Woolf says, George Eliot is the great mouthpiece of woman's sensibility, it is not without significance that she has based her ethics on an emotion towards the past. Hetty Sorrel was worthless because she was without this emotion.

> Hetty could have cast all her life behind her, and never cared to be reminded of it again. I think she had no feeling at all towards the old house, and did not like the Jacob's Ladder and the long

row of hollyhocks in the garden better than other flowers – perhaps not so well.

Maggie Tulliver sacrifices her happiness because she feels she cannot be disloyal to her past.

It is not only educated women who have this cult of the past. I once listened to two old creatures of the lower middle class (the widows, I should imagine, of rich tradesmen) making friends in the lounge of an hotel. They had discovered that long ago they had both lived in Sussex, and were interchanging reminiscences; or, rather, they were hurling them at each other's heads, for there is a tough, unplastic quality about the conversation of the uneducated, and the remarks of one talker never seem to modify those of the other. It was something like this: –

First Old Woman: Oh, I'm very fond of Sussex.
Second Old Woman: Yaas, yaas, yaas. Oh, I know Sussex very well.
F.O.W.: Yaas, yaas, yaas. But all these places are changing. Oh, I know Sussex very well.
S.O.W.: Yaas. I used to be very fond of Hastings.
F.O.W.: Yaas, yaas, yaas.
S.O.W.: I used to live there when I was a girl. But all these places are springing up so you wouldn't know them.
F.O.W.: Yaas. I used to live in Bexhill. I lived there in my husband's lifetime. Oh, I'm very fond of Sussex.

It was all very dull and unemotional, and they might just as well have been shouting remarks to each other across a slum street about a smoking flue, or the price of margarine. But the emotion was there all the same, as I was to discover the following day. It was Christmas Eve, and the 'loud speaker' was singing Christmas carols to the visitors as they sat drinking their tea in the lounge. I happened to be near one of the old women from Sussex, and I watched her face as she listened to 'Hark the Herald Angels Sing'. She looked so rapt, so profoundly moved, as to be almost beautiful. But, I feel convinced, it was memories that were singing to her, and not angels. And they were not singing of the birth of Christ – unless Christ was born at Bexhill, in her husband's lifetime. In the same way, a great many women go to church. But are they all *really* devout? The Prayer Book tells us the *Phronema sarkos* is 'not subject to the Law of God'. I suspect that the majority of them go to church because they find in the hymns and liturgy an oblique expression of the wisdom of their bodies and the sensibility of their minds. And while the exquisite academic voice of Archbishop Cranmer, the treble and bass of the four Evangelists, and all the hymns ancient and modern are repeating: –

>The happy, mournful stories,
>The lamentable glories
>Of the great crucified King,

they are thinking of themselves. No, not *thinking*; rather, swaying backwards and forwards, like seaweed, in a bitter-sweet sea of memories and hopes and vague yearning. In fact, they have no right to be in church at all; unless Christ and Time are one. Perhaps they are. Euripides calls time the 'great *daimon*'; and the difference between a *daimon* and a god, says Miss Jane Harrison, is that a *daimon* is bound to the ceaselessly revolving wheel of birth, death, resurrection. A *daimon* is an impersonation of the year and its fruits. And I suppose Time is an impersonation of the actual process to which the *daimon* is subject. He has also, by a cruel irony, taken over some of the attributes of Mother Earth – the bountiful, the benign. What Sophocles says about time, in the passage from the 'Ajax' I have already quoted, might be an echo of these words of Æschylus about earth: –

>...Earth who brings all things to life
>And rears and takes again into her womb.

The conception of Time is a cruel substitute for that of Mother Earth. It is as if Oreithyia had died, and her little children had suddenly found themselves with no one to turn to but their father, the wind.

However, if only the Earth had turned perpendicularly on its axis, the body would have kept its secret to itself and the fear of Time would not have troubled our dreams. Owing to the Earth's tilt we have strongly contrasted seasons, which tread on each other's heels – a pageant striking enough and of frequent enough recurrence to focus even the *distrait*, restless eye of primitive man. And from this model – the cycle of the seasons – he draws the wavering stippled outline of his first picture of life as a whole, and of his own fate. On Jupiter, where the axis is nearly perpendicular to the planet's orbit, the seasons, I believe, are separated from each other not by months but by years, so if ever Jupiter comes to be inhabited, the burden of its songs and ballads will not be time and change. I am not supposing that its inhabitants will be immortal, but only suggesting that their emotional focus will not be their own mortality. It may be that they will take eternity for their bogey, just as we have taken time; for, being men, they will certainly have bogies. But they will not think of themselves in terms of the 'beautiful and death-struck year', as wingless seeds to whom the Spring calls in vain. And when their hearts swell, as they surely will, in an agony of self-pity, of self-pity and of pity for their friends, they will not cry: –

> Even as are the generations of the leaves such are those likewise of men.

Homer puts these words into the mouth of Glaucus, the son of Hippolochus – a man. In fact, it is indisputable that nearly all the great tragic utterances about time, and its corollaries, change and death, have been made by men. It is, nevertheless, only the poets, and not the average man, who are haunted by these conceptions. But they do haunt all women. As a general rule, it is love that makes men unhappy, and time that makes women so. And if Time be a *daimon*, it is natural that this should be so. Were not women the chief mourners for Thammuz and Adonaïs? How much more should they mourn for Time. One of the duties of slaves is to mourn their master, and women are the slaves of Time. Has he not branded their bodies with his mark – the periodicity of the moon?

Gothic Dreams

Thanks to *Northanger Abbey*, the ingenious Mrs Radcliffe is apt to be regarded as a writer who was admired exclusively by foolish young ladies. But Catherine Morland, when she shuddered and squealed over *The Mysteries of Udolpho*, was in excellent company. Learned old gentlemen like Joseph Warton sat up all night to finish it, and it was the favourite book in their youth of the great poets of the Romantic Movement. Nowadays we prefer Mr Edgar Wallace and Mrs Agatha Christie. But it is doubtful whether these writers will have as much influence on the poets of the coming generation as Mrs Radcliffe had on Scott and Byron and Shelley. Mrs Radcliffe, though undoubtedly a goose, was almost hysterically in tune with the 'movement', and there is an echo in her books of nearly every modulation in eighteenth-century sensibility. Her heroine (she has only one) is Clarissa Harlowe, who was buried in Blair's Grave, and rose again in a dress of the Macpherson tartan, in floods of tears, and murmuring between her sobs odes to the Alps, or the evening star, or her dead canary. But it was the heroine's bloodcurdling adventures in a Gothic castle that constituted Mrs Radcliffe's chief claim on the attention of her intellectual contemporaries; for in those days the souls of the cultured found in 'thrillers' their most satisfying food. So if Mr Wallace wants to play the same rôle as Mrs Radcliffe he must entirely alter his procedure, and confine the activities of his crooks and sleuths to coprolitic *monologues intérieurs* against a background by Picasso or Braque.

It was a happy idea of Mr Rialto's to call his book on the *Schauerromantik The Haunted Castle*. The Gothic castle was much more than a fashionable background for adventure stories; it was, I believe, the symbol of the eighteenth-century hunger for the 'sublime', which produced Mrs Radcliffe and was the cause of her being admired by serious people. Mr Rialto provides us with a minute description of the castle's architecture, a list of its architects from Horace Walpole to Poe, and a complete inventory of its furniture; ghosts in armour, moping owl, phantom voices, and a score of other grisly items, most of which he traces back to Shakespeare. But in his examination of the sources of the general *Stimmung* he omits to mention the celebrated description of a Gothic church in Congreve's *Mourning Bride*. And in his list of the demoniac lords of the castle there is another curious omission – that of the greatest of the race, Heathcliff of

Wuthering Heights. Mr Rialto's learning and industry are immense, but his book is a trifle indigested. It would gain in interest, though it might possibly lose in 'soundness', if the facts were threaded on something one could call an 'argument'.

If the Gothic castle really stands for the 'sublime', then the eighteenth century can be regarded as a Childe Roland who never came to the Dark Tower. But it tried very hard. Even Pope nearly tried. In a letter to Mrs Cowper he confesses that he has long wanted to write a fairy-tale with the technique of a dream. This was rank heresy and almost looks as if he were swerving from his allegiance to the tenets of Hobbes. But, as if frightened by his own boldness, he draws back with the reservation 'provided there be an apparent moral to it.' The *Zeitgeist*, however, and the particular bend of a writer's quill are apt to play strange tricks with the first conception of a book, and if Pope had actually written his fairy-tale I do not think it would have been of a kind to make Hobbes turn in his grave. In the meantime a fresh breed was growing up. If one wants to understand the beginnings of the Romantic Movement one cannot do better than study the *obiter dicta* of Herder. I admit it is difficult to believe that there were any Germans in the eighteenth century. But the fact remains that Herder, though a German, was born in 1744, and that he said a novel ought to be like a dream. As it happens, the first of the 'Gothic' romances, Horace Walpole's *Castle of Otranto*, actually had its origin in a dream; for, in spite of Hobbes, the eighteenth-century writers spent as many hours out of the twenty-four as the Elizabethans or the Lake Poets in riding on chimæras, and even Dr Johnson's dreams must have been much more 'Gothic' than the Runic Odes that stirred his bile. Perhaps the 'sublime', which such critics as Hurd and the Wartons found in Spenser and Ariosto but not in the ancients, and which they wished to see produced in the work of their contemporaries, was a dream-like atmosphere. Burke says that *terror* is the 'common stock of everything that is sublime'; and in our dreams we have often even more terrifying adventures than Emily in *The Mysteries of Udolpho*.

The 'Gothic age', which means, roughly, the Middle Ages, was fixed upon as the right background for the sublime. Now the Gothic revival is generally identified with the so-called birth of the historical imagination, supposed to have taken place towards the end of the eighteenth century. This expression 'historical imagination', as used by the critics, seems to cover three distinct perceptions: a sense of the past, a sense of period, and the historical imagination proper. But Lucretius had a magnificent historical imagination, and a sense of the past was exquisitely expressed as early as the fifteenth century in Villon's 'Ballade des dames du temps jadis'. As for the sense of period, though it was certainly one of the pioneers of the Gothic revival – Gray – who first possessed it, it was for the Tudor, not for the mediæval period. In short, not only should I deny that the Gothic revival was the result of any of these three perceptions, but I should even doubt whether, at any rate in the beginning, it had anything to do with them. Certainly not one of them functions in *The Castle of Otranto*. What the Gothic revival in literature really sprang from was a sense that the past was frightening, a bad dream – the *Gothic* past, that is to say. But it is because it is Gothic that it is frightening rather than because it is the past. Scott in his interesting essay on Horace Walpole commends him for having chosen a Gothic background for *The Castle of Otranto*, because he thus produces in the mind of the reader terror, and hence credulity. He compares the terror to that induced by sleeping in an old house in a room hung with trappings of the past.

> The gigantic and preposterous figures dimly visible in the defaced tapestry...the dimly seen pictures of ancient knights, renowned for their valour and perhaps for their crimes...and to crown all, the feeling that carries us back to ages of feudal power and papal superstition, join together to excite a corresponding sensation of supernatural awe, if not of terror.

But why were the Middle Ages considered more frightening than any other period? Hurd said that the 'Gothic' writers were more successful than the ancients in producing the sublime because of 'the superior solemnity of their superstitions.'...Scott's 'papal superstition' again. I suspect that the Middle Ages were frightening because they were pre-eminently Catholic Ages. For many generations the Church of Rome had exercised a sinister fascination over the minds of Englishmen, at once repelling and attracting them. In the Caroline Poets we find this two-edged emotion at an early stage. To Herrick, the Roman ritual is merely a pretty, comic, though slightly uncanny, game. It is white magic, or, rather, pale green. In fact, it is faerie. The fairies, he says, do 'much affect the Papacie': –

> For sanctity, they have, to these,
> Their curious Copes and Surplices
> Of cleanest Cobweb hanging by
> In their Religious Vesterie.

But to Marvell, though still faerie, it has already become more sinister, and the nuns of 'Appleton House' might have a stall for their 'pastes and balms' in Goblin Market. And so by degrees we come to Lewis's fiendish monk and nineteenth-century 'diablerie'. This is not to suggest that the craving for the sublime sprang entirely from a sense of the *ambivalence* of Rome. It is merely pushing the symbol a stage back and discovering behind the Gothic castle a Popish church. What lay behind *that* would take a psycho-analyst to discover; and as the patient would be a couple of centuries instead of an individual, Professor Freud himself might find it a nut too hard to crack.

It is possible that a Popish church was the origin of the most famous of all the eighteenth-century Gothic castles – Strawberry Hill. On Horace Walpole's first visit to Paris the monument that interests him more than any other is the Convent of the Chartreux. While he admires its architecture, its atmosphere sends agreeable shudders down his spine – 'its large and obscure hall looks like a combination-room for some hellish council.' In short, he reacts to its Catholicism in the typical English way. He sees in it, however, domestic possibilities: 'soften the terms and mellow the uncouth horror that reigns here but a little, and 'tis a charming solitude...' In fact, 'tis Strawberry.

Well, if this is the true history of Strawberry, it can serve as an allegory of the fate of the Pre-Romantics. They sought the sublime and found the ridiculous. Perhaps the explanation of their failure lies in Pope's reservation, 'provided there be an apparent moral to it.' In any case, Childe Roland did not come to the Dark Tower till the publication in 1798 of *Lyrical Ballads*. And both Tintern Abbey and the baronial hall in 'Christabel' are Gothic castles; while Kubla Khan's 'stately pleasure-dome' is a palace in a dream.

Bedside Books

Above all, they must not be dull. Dullness (*pace* Pope) is *not* a soporific. If it were, it would have its uses, and serious modern novels might live as lullabies. But dullness *per se* has never yet put any one to sleep, and when we nod in church, the poppies tangled in garnered piety are the cause and not the parson's homily, and if Jeremy Taylor himself were preaching on Christmas Day, and his text was *Nevertheless the Dimness,* we should not be a wink less drowsy. Even a detective story is more soothing than a dull book. *Suave mari* – a detective story may sometimes be read in bed. To extract the last drop of sweetness from this delightful hour, we must be conscious of our bed as well as of our book, and a detective story emphasises the conceit that our bed is a hare's form, a warm secret refuge from hunters and hounds – while outside our sanctuary there is terror and flight and the surging enemy, mute and terrible.

> Suave, mari magno turbantibus aequora ventis,
> E terra magnum alterius spectare laborem.

These lines make it easy to fancy that Lucretius as well as we felt the charm of lying in bed, awake but not wakeful...in a cave in the cliffs where shipwrecked mariners have lighted a fire and are returning thanks to Neptune for their great deliverance, and the sea roaring outside is the 'splendour and smoke and din of Rome'. Or, perhaps, the sound of the sea was made out of country noises – the soughing of the wind in the trees, the hooting of owls; noises that drown the sound of Time and enable us, as we listen to them, to be lying in bed in the reign of Rameses II, or of Cyrus the Great, or of Hiram, King of Tyre. They are the sounds to which we like best to think of Lucretius falling asleep; for those of us who are lovers of the *De Rerum Natura* are *ipso facto* lovers of Lucretius the man, and welcome any foreshortening of the centuries between us. No shadow of Virgil falls across the *Aeneid* (according to the medieval legend he was a wizard, and a wizard cannot cast a shadow), but the *De Rerum Natura* is charged with Lucretius, and we are frequently brought into so sharp and intimate a contact with him that it resembles an electric shock. For instance, we can be as certain as of our own existence that, in one of the last twenty Aprils of the Republic, a man in a toga, called Titus Lucretius Carus, stood gazing intently at an Italian landscape. In the distance, what his *eyes* saw was a motionless spot of white on a green hill, but his brain told him that it was dew-drawn sheep nibbling their way across the happy pasture, and lambs frisking in the sun. Then out came his tablets, and he made a note for a possible simile to illustrate the thesis 'though the first-beginnings of all things are in motion, yet the sum is seen to rest in supreme repose'. It might also be a simile of the contrast between the past, as it appears to us, and as it really was. And when the past happens to be the inner life of an infinitely great poet who lived very long ago, how can we have the presumption to hope that it will not be white, and motionless, and very distant? And yet – a grace far, far beyond our deserts – here is the print of a human foot on 'the pathless haunts of the Pierides'.

So we can be sure that Lucretius lay in bed and read. . .Epicurus, I suppose. But we must not compare the bed of the superb Lucretius to a hare's form. Rather (on the nights when Vulcan had turned the key on Venus), it was the *intermundia*, the windless abode of the Epicurean gods – an easy metamorphosis for a bed, and Tennyson's paraphrase of *intermundia*, 'the lucid interspace of world and world', might, out of its context, serve as a description of the hour between walking and sleeping.

> Apparet divum numen sedesque quietae
> Quas neque concutiunt venti nec nubila nimbis
> Aspergunt neque nix acri concreta pruina
> Cana cadens violat semperque innubilis aether
> Integit, et large diffuso lumine rident.

Great magnanimous Lucretius! While he lived, his sojourns in that place were infrequent and of short duration; but now. . . *immortali aevo summa cum pace fruatur*, may he enjoy his immortality with perfect peace.

But it is not for us to fall asleep on the knees of the gods; and conceits are not the only opiate – for instance, there is music. Let our book, then, have some of the qualities of music. But they must be the qualities that music has for the unmusical, what we want are dreams, and sound without sense. It is the *Iliad* of all books that is the most like music. It is also of all books the most melancholy, and Lamb has shown us that a poetical melancholy is a seemly mood on which to fall asleep. Here is the quintessential perfume of the sensitive plant of all the solar systems; a perfume lost in space among gorgeous insensate suns. The terrible war-cries of Ajax and Hector, the clash of bronze swords, the voices of the slayer and the slain, die away into an exquisitely melodious, infinitely melancholy echo. And one asks – as Homer, perhaps, means one should – What does it matter, the waste of all this chivalry and high endeavour and eloquence and rage and love? And the answer seems to be: It matters no more than when 'reapers over against each other drive their swaths through a rich man's field of wheat or barley'.

It may be that this musical melancholy is partly due to Homer's way of showing us the action through a prism, one of the facets of which is the future. At times the story seems to be happening as we read. And then he suddenly pulls us up and reminds us that really it all happened very long ago, that we have heard it all hundreds of times before, and know the end as well as he. Hence, like the God of Molina the Jesuit, we view the human drama with *scientia media*, knowledge of what is going to happen. This is not the same as the famous tragic irony of Sophocles, which springs from the contrast between the *scientia media* of the spectator and the blindness to futurity of the characters themselves. In the *Iliad* it is not only we, the spectators, who have *scientia media*; there are moments when the heroes have it also. The two great protagonists, Hector and Achilles, are aware: Hector, that Troy is doomed to fall, and his wife to be sold into captivity; Achilles, that 'he must perish in deep-soiled Troy, far from his native land'. But the *scientia media* of Hector and Achilles is not the same as that expounded by Molina. Molina invented the conception to reconcile God's omniscience with man's free-will. It is the focus of two eyes looking through different lenses; but the eyes do not belong to the same person – one is God's, the other is man's. Hector and Achilles, however, do not share their optic glass with God, and it is in their own vision that prescience is adjusted to free-will. Achilles has the choice of two alternatives, either to continue fighting the Trojans and to have as his reward death but imperishable fame; or else to sail back to Thessaly and have a long life, but an inglorious one. And he knows from the outset what his choice will be, for in Book I he begins his prayer to Thetis:

Mother, seeing thou did'st bear me to so brief a span of life.

But this prescience does not affect his actions, nor does it result in fatalism, for it is not merely a conviction based on a knowledge of his own character, it is *scientia media* – a sudden focusing of two divergent points of view. It is the same with Hector. His knowledge of futurity does not prevent him from doing his best to beat the

Greeks. And there are even moments when he forgets what he has seen through *scientia media*, for in Book VIII he prays 'with *good hope* to Zeus and all the gods to drive from hence these dogs borne onward by the fates'.

Through *scientia media* there are moments when the *Iliad* has a fourth dimension. Thebes was built by music; but one of the walls of Ilium *is* music.

But we have decided that our bedside-book must be music for the unmusical. To the musical great music is rarely soothing. And some of us cannot lie still under great poetry.

> Even as when in heaven the stars about the bright moon shine clear to see, when the air is windless and all the peaks appear and the tall headlands and glades, and from heaven breaketh open the infinite air and all stars are seen, and the shepherd's heart is glad.

Oh that shepherd is the Homeric similes! He is like the little human figures in a Corot. As Corot's figures turn a landscape into poetry, so Homer's shepherd turns it into music, as if we heard his flute.

Then the great scene in the last book, when Priam comes as a suppliant to Achilles and conjures him to remember his own father and to be merciful:

> Then Priam spoke, and entreated him by saying: 'Bethink thee, god-like Achilles, of thy father that is of like years with me, on the grievous pathway of old age. Him, it may be the dwellers round about him are entreating evilly, nor is there any to ward from him ruin and bane. Nevertheless, while he hears of thee as yet alive he rejoices in his heart, and hopes, withal, day after day that he shall see his dear son returning from Troy-land. But I, I am utterly unblest, since I begat sons the best men in wide Troy-land, but declare unto thee that none of them is left...Now of the greater part had impetuous Ares unstrung the knees, and he who was yet left and guarded city and men, him slewest thou but now as he fought for his country, even Hector. For his sake come I unto the ships of the Achaians, that I may win him back from thee, and I bring with me untold ransom. Yea, fear thou the gods, Achilles, and have compassion on me, even me, bethinking thee of they father – Lo, I am yet more piteous than he, and have braved what none other man on earth has braved before, to stretch forth my hand toward the face of the slayer of my sons.'

Thus spake he, and stirred within Achilles desire to make lament for his father. And he touched the old man's hand and gently moved him back. And as they both bethought them of their dead, so Priam for manslaying Hector wept sore, as he was fallen before Achilles's feet, and Achilles wept for his own father, and now again for Patroclus, and their moan went up throughout the house.

The Black Prince, when his prisoner, the King of France, sat down to meat, waited on him himself – a *beau geste* which has caught the fancy of history. But here is something infinitely more moving than the conventions of chivalry. They are only a passing fashion; but the great moments when the grief for youth cut off in its flower and for old age left with none to tend it, and the grief for old age falling asleep and leaving youth with none to counsel it, and the grief for our friends who are beneath the earth are merged into one great movement of self-pity, so wide that it embraces our enemies, and Priam and Peleus, and Hector and Patroclus, and we ourselves, are blurred into one person – these moments are not of yesterday nor of to-day. And yet they are but moments, gone in a flash. It is only by great music that they are caught and prolonged. And wise Achilles, old Cheiron's pupil, knew their fragility, so he ordered his servants to cover the body of Hector, lest at the sight of it both Priam's wrath and his own should spring up afresh.

No more than when 'reapers drive their swaths through a rich man's field of wheat or barley'. . .Is a great poet, then, a cheat, whose scales have false weights?

But see! The sensitive plant is drinking the sun. We have read all night.

We have discovered, then, that our book must be like music, but not music of a shattering beauty. What about *The Anatomy of Melancholy*? The A-na-tomy of Me-lan-choly. The syllables are made of poppy and mandragora. Here is music for the unmusical – a volume of sound, a tissue of dreams. *Facta est immensi copia mundi*, the cornucopia of the world is spilt at our feet – *stars, suns, moons, metals, sweet-smelling flowers*, like starfish strewing the Christ Church lawn round the kind old conjurer of melancholy; a daintier litter than the carcases of anatomised beasts that surrounded the other Democritus – Burton's toy and Lucretius's master – in *his* search for a cure for melancholy; but, as drugs, probably no more efficacious. It would, indeed, be a stubborn melancholy that would not melt at a glimpse of the great bird Ruck. But the other remedies in Burton's pharmacopoeia – Indian pictures made of feathers, for instance – set us wondering if he realised the gravity of the complaint for which he was prescribing. But this is unfair. Burton belongs to the school of leeches who hold that every flower upon the daedal earth secretes a juice that will heal melancholy, if only we can extract it. The other school turn the cold shoulder to Pandora, for they know that, in spite of her bedizening, her womb is the very nursery of the seeds of melancholy. All the same, one cannot help suspecting that Burton himself had never suffered from anything more serious than the medieval *accidia*, that intermittent irascibility and impatience of the tune to which one's life is set, which was found chiefly among monks and clerks, and, to this day, I am told, affects the atmosphere of the common-rooms of Oxford and Cambridge. For one thing, Burton was, relatively speaking, pure. As he writes of the protean twists of lust, of the madness it engenders, of all the spells and charms it has by heart, and of all its lovely masks, his slick pen never sputters. It is true he writes with a certain complacency. But it is the complacency of the collector pinning yet another specimen caught in Ovid or Petronius into his box of butterflies. Maps move him much more than women's looks. And, except for an occasional dig at the knights of Cupid, foolish young gallants whose only art is to wear their clothes with a good grace (Burton, it must be remembered, was a Fellow of Christ Church), he writes without indignation. Temperament – the hall-mark (hell-mark) of Lucretius and St Augustine and Donne and Baudelaire – some tragic discord between the spirit and the flesh, which gives to style the great Roman quality of *gravitas*, and which makes nobler literature than ever harmony does, had never tortured Burton.

There is a legend to the effect that Lucretius was given a love philtre which caused recurrent fits of madness, and that in his lucid intervals he wrote the *De Rerum Natura*. Perhaps this is an allegory rather than a legend. Lucretius maintains that the only cause of melancholy is the fear of the gods, and its corollary, the fear of death. If a man will apply to this poison the antidote of sovereign reason, he will recognise the operation of Law in Nature, and, knowing that everything has a natural cause, will attain to the supreme happiness of being able to look at all things with a mind at peace – at the way of an eagle in the air, at the way of a serpent upon a rock, at the way of a ship in the midst of the sea. But could Lucretius look with a mind at peace at the way of a man with a maid? If you think he could, then re-read his description of Mavors in the lap of Venus.

Burton had read Lucretius, and sometimes quotes from him. But never has one great imagination been less influenced by another, for the Sirens were the only fabulous birds in all mythologies of the world against whose song he had waxed his ears. The song of the Sirens, Jane Harrison tells us, is true knowledge. And yet, once, in the splendid antithetical passage where he swings between Democritus and Heraclitus in alternate laughter and tears over the follies and woes of superstition, pity and indignation have made his voice so resonant that we can almost fancy it will vibrate back through the centuries and reach the ears of Lucretius. But this is not Burton's usual voice – and why should it be? We go to him for exquisite fantastic entertainment – sea-shells gathered on inland mountains and mandrake wine. But Lucretius and he have one strand in their imagination that is the same. Each is haunted, as Pindar was before them, by gold and purple – as symbols, and for their own sake. Peacocks, potentates, pageants, gold of Ophir, Tyrian coverlets – it is the *lustre* of the earth, the *glamour* of pomp and power. But to Burton they are cures for melancholy, while Lucretius holds that they cannot even benefit our bodies, how much less, then, our minds.

But why pit old Burton against Lucretius? As Lucretius said of himself, in relation to Epicurus:

Why need the swallow contend with swans?

And we, in our turn, will not make an eagle contend with a. . .what shall we say? I was once driving in an omnibus along one of the interminable semi-rural roads of Hampstead, drowned in melancholy. . . no, it cannot have been melancholy, it must have been *accidia*, for it was suddenly exorcised by a voice; and Odysseus himself can never have turned a deaf ear to a stranger and more amusing one. With a jerk of delight I came to my senses. The conductor and grown-up passengers were smiling indulgently, the children were jogging up and down in their seats with glee. And the source of all this pleasure was the owner of an amusing voice – a green crimson-flecked parrot whom an old lady was carrying in a Sheraton cage. His expression as he contemplated us, his head a little on one side, was humorous and full of meaning. All the same, I had a disconcerting feeling that the creature's expression had really nothing to do with his reactions; that he was wearing, in fact, a comic mask; and from my previous acquaintance with parrots, I was aware that, could I have looked up at him from below, an hiatus would have revealed the clumsy adjustment of the false nose. And that completely spherical eye – a circle of tangerine round an olive-green iris, a gaudy target at a Lilliputian fair, with the pupil for the bull's-eye – could it be a *real* organ of sight? But suddenly the iris started quivering and vibrating, and the pupil began slowly to expand, so that the very process of seeing was made visible. I thought of the terrible stylised Eye painted on the heavens. Just like that must it suddenly have quivered and vibrated, on the First Day, when it saw that the light was good. But who could guess the parrot's thoughts, as he contemplated us out of that spherical eye? Was he wondering if the cherries on our lips would be worth the pecking, or the flowers stamped on our muslins? And then I nearly squealed with pleasure, and I could not help feeling flattered, although I knew it was only mimicry of the most engaging trick of Fido or Dash (what a dominant personality, so to impress his *cachet* on his surroundings as to turn our jumpers into sprigged muslins, our pekinese into Dash, the spaniel!) – through the bars of his cage he offered me his horny three-pronged claw. Yes, I had nearly forgotten his cage, but it was very important. He was a parrot in a Sheraton cage (a prettier cage than Christ Church), and that made him different from an ordinary parrot, and embossed him into a bas-relief slightly above the level of Nature, so that, instead of a bird, he was a thaumaturgical toy – a Punch and Judy straight from Fairyland; or, rather, from the country that marches with Fairyland, where works of art grow petals and feathers, and birds and flowers are Indian pictures, and where Oxford dons are 'fantastic old great men'.

But my simile is growing Homeric. We must not forget that we are in bed, and the Sheraton cage is covered up for the night with a crimson cloth, and Burton is lulling us to sleep. Do not fear to be distracted by too great a diversity, or cloyed by a surfeit of erudition. The old man, in spite of his innocence, has dabbled in the black arts, and he binds with his spells popes and pornographists and geographers and Fathers till they are as 'besotted as birds with henbane', and dance to his piping. And though the words belong to Aeneas Silvius, or Levinus Lemnius, or Ovidius Naso, the voice is always Burton's. Under all the extravagance and outlandishness there flows something as peaceful and familiar and English as his own Leicestershire river.

> But this is still and quiet: and if so the *reader* catch no Fish, yet he hath a wholesome walk to the brook side, pleasant shade by the sweet silver streams; he hath good air, and sweet smells of fine fresh meadow flowers, he hears the melodious harmony of birds,

he sees the swans, herons, ducks, water-hens, coots, and many other fowl, with their brood, which he thinketh better than the noise of hounds, or blast of horns, and all the sport they can make.

Better than the noise of hounds or blast of horns! We are back, then, in our hare's form. Put out the light.

NOTES AND APPENDIX

Abbreviations

HM	Hope Mirrlees
JH	Jane Ellen Harrison
M&T	*Moods and Tensions: Seventeen Poems* (privately printed, unknown date, after *Poems* and post-1961)
M&T76	*Moods and Tensions* (Amate Press, 1976)
Poems	*Poems* (Cape Town: Gothic Printing, unknown date, before 1961)

Where possible, composition dates are provided.

Commentary on *Paris*
Julia Briggs

Note entries and bracketed references are keyed to the line number in which they appear.

Dedication   'To Our Lady of Paris in recognition of graces granted'. 'Our Lady of Paris' is both the Virgin Mary and the great cathedral dedicated to her on the Ile-de-la-Cité, at the centre of Paris, with an echo of the prayer 'Ave Maria, gratia plena' ('Hail Mary, full of grace' – see 444). The frame suggests that of a votive plaque such as might be hung in a church. From the outset, Paris is addressed as a woman.

1   'holophrase', a single word standing for a phrase, sentence or complex of ideas, and according to Jane Harrison (JH) characteristic of an early stage of language development (*Themis* 473–5). 'I want' can also mean 'I lack'. 'Holophrase' puns on 'hollow phrase'.

2   Métro line from Montparnasse to Montmartre, now line 12.

3–6   Brand names on métro posters: 'Zig-Zag', type of cigarette paper, advertised with the head of a 'Zouave', an Algerian soldier (and anticipating the poem's zig-zag direction through the city); 'Lion Noir' (black lion), a brand of shoe polish; 'Cacao Blooker', Dutch make of drinking chocolate. These introduce themes of empire and of *négritude* (blackness), further linked with 'Black-figured vases' (550–480 BC), found in Etruscan burial chambers.

7–9   'Rue du Bac', 'Solférino' and 'Chambre des Députés' (now 'Assemblée Nationale'), the three most northerly stations on the Nord-Sud line south of the river (rue du Bac is next to rue de Beaune, where HM lived while writing the poem). 'Solférino', named for a French victory over Austria in Italy (1859). From 1832, the Chambre des Députés was the French lower house of government. 'Dubonnet', brand of fortified wine advertised in métro tunnels, HM's curved brackets suggesting the walls of the métro on which the posters appeared.

10   'Brekekekek coax coax', chorus of Aristophanes' *The Frogs* (405 BC) in the underworld (also suggesting rattling wooden carriages in the métro). 'Frogs', British slang for the French, used in letters between HM and JH.

12–13   'The Scarlet Woman' appears to St John on the Greek island of Patmos (Revelation 17.3–6). 'Byrrh', another fortified wine, advertised with a poster of a woman dressed in scarlet, playing a drum and shouting (see Cocteau 49, 38 for 'BYRRH' and St John as witness). In the Hogarth edition, 'St' is inserted before 'John' by Virginia Woolf's hand on 160 copies.

14   'Are you getting off here, madame?' standard polite phrase for making one's own way off a crowded métro car or bus.
15–16   'Those who weigh themselves [up] often, know themselves well. Those who know themselves well, stay healthy', motto on station scales.
17   The speaker alights at the first station north of the river: Place de la Concorde, a huge square on the Right Bank, formerly used for royal events, the guillotine during the revolution, etc. 'Concorde' means 'agreement', introducing the theme of the peace process (MacMillan, passim).
20–2   The spaced-out layout of these lines imitates that of the Tuileries gardens, with gaps left for the basins on the central axis at either end. The poem slows down, changing direction from south > north (vertical movement on the page) to west > east (horizontal).
23–6   The little boys riding on a carousel in the Tuileries (out of use during World War I) become soldiers, their hands sticky from the mud of the trenches (anticipates lines 89–92, 275–6).
27–9   The pigeons appear to be joined to the statues in the Tuileries, while the statues look 'two-dimensional' (273, 403). One, looking over her shoulder, suggests Watteau's *Le Départ pour Cythere* (properly, *L'Embarcation pour Cythère*, 1717, in the Louvre), in which those leaving for Cytherea (the island of Venus) look back.
30–4   Some statues are of nymphs. Louis Pasteur (1822–95) developed a vaccine against rabies (Sacha Guitry's play *Pasteur* was running in Paris in early 1919. A métro station on the Nord-Sud line had been named after him). 'Gauls', the French, as warriors or soldiers. The Nymphs' soft mouths also suggest female genitals ('nymphae', labia minora); their 'bite' may refer to venereal disease.
34–9   Leon Gambetta, national hero and Minister for War during the German siege of Paris, announced the Third Republic in September 1870 (in the presence of the 1919 Prime Minister Georges Clemençeau – the first buried reference to him). Gambetta's statue in a frock coat (now in the square Edouar-Vailant, 20éme) then stood at the base of a seventy-five-foot monumental pyramid in front of the Louvre, with a winged 'Genius of France' leaning over him. HM imagines a red stud (his *legion d'honneur* rosette) in a button-hole (*boutonnière* is slang for anus), suggesting a possible intimacy between these two figures.
36   *tutoiement*, an intimate form of address (*tu*) employed by couples.
37   'But it makes sense.'
38   Esprit Français, 'Spirit of France'. The winged 'Genius' on the Gambetta monument.
40–2   'Secrets', defined by four terms set in a square that play between English and French senses: 'exquisite' (Fr. *exquis*); 'significant' (Fr. *significatif*); 'fade', a verb in English, an adjective in French meaning tasteless or insipid; 'plastic' (*plastique*), malleable, moulded, flowing, often applied to sculpture or the visual arts, a favourite word for HM (see lines 112, 289; HM's novel *Madeleine*, vii).
43–50   (Exquisite / significant secrets) Of ... Goya's painting of the

Duchess of Alba (1795, near the end of the war between France, Germany and Spain) depicts her as tall and slender, a pyramid, resembling both the Eiffel Tower and Gambetta's monument. Red ribbons in her hair and on her dress echo his red stud. She seems drugged, and, like him, is pointing, in her case to a small (Maltese) dog at her feet, as if directing the Magi to the infant Jesus at Epiphany. HM and JH may have seen this painting in Madrid in 1916; Goya was fashionable with the French avant-garde.

51   (Significant / plastic secrets) Of . . . On the top of the Gambetta monument was a figure of Democracy riding on a lion. *Lysistrata*, heroine of a play by Aristophanes (411 BC), persuaded the women of Athens to end the war with Sparta by going on sexual strike. The play was staged at the Marigny Theatre, and another play inspired by it, *La grève des femmes*, was also running in Paris in spring 1919.

54   ('Fade' or fading secrets) Of . . .

55–6   From the Place du Carrousel, the Arc de Triomphe is visible at the far end of the Champs Elysées. Caesar (whose statue stands in the Tuileries) scorns dreams in Shakespeare's play.

58   Salle Caillebotte, room in the Musée du Luxembourg, hung with French Impressionist paintings. The painter Gustave Caillebotte's unique collection of these was at first refused by the French government, but from 1896 most of them were on display.

59   The journey through Paris continues.

60–1   'The Etoile', the *place* at the top of the Champs Elysées, at the centre of the fashionable west side, named 'etoile' (star) because twelve avenues radiated from it. 'The Bois', (Bois de Boulogne), public park at its western edge.

62   In J-K. Huysmans' decadent novel *A Rebours* (1884), Des Esseintes has the shell of a living tortoise encrusted with jewels.

63   'Spinario', Roman statue in bronze (first century BC) in the Museo dei Conservatori in Rome. Renaissance copies abound, some in the Louvre.

64–5   Juliette Récamier, famous beauty, and lover of the poet Chateaubriand (362). 'Discalceated', a rare word for 'barefooted', as she appears in a portrait (1800) by Jacques-Louis David (291), in the Louvre. *De nos jours*, of our time.

67–8   'Saunters' suggests the *flâneur*, stroller or wanderer, a characteristic Parisian type; 'rue Saint-Honoré', old street meandering from east to west parallel with the river (Chateaubriand lived at no. 374). 'Grand Seigneur', a great lord. Brittany, the westernmost region of France, introduces a tour of the provinces.

69   Auvergnat, hot chestnut-seller, native of the Auvergne, the mountainous area of central France. Celtic Brittany and the Gallic Auvergne represent old traditional French stock. Many nineteenth-century Parisians came from Brittany and central France (Higonnet 77).

71–6   Paris was often pictured as a city of peasants, and its *quartiers* thought of as villages, especially by the Surrealists (see Louis Aragon's later *Le Paysan de Paris*, 1926). Many Paris houses have large gates, providing glimpses of 'Hidden courts' decorated with classical figures such as 'putti', though the 'Little gods' could be the city's artists, musicians and writers.

77   The Gallic cock is a national symbol. The cock wakens the farmer, usually banishing ghosts, though here it becomes the ghost of Hesiod, an early Greek poet who 'sang' (as the cock does) of country life in his *Works and Days* (both denied to the dead). 'Acheron', was one of the four rivers of the classical underworld/afterlife.

83   That is, peace; also the 'Eniautos Daimon', whose birth and death correspond to seasonal change, the central theme of JH's *Themis*.

85–7   The Spirit of the Year is laid out, corpse-like, in fields whose ploughed furrows ('nos sillons') suggest the fluted drapery of archaic Greek statues, as well as the trenches of World War I.

89–92   Children hung with amulets (good luck charms, to protect from danger) are also reincarnated soldiers (as at line 23; see Cocteau 41). *Pigeon vole* (literally, 'pigeon, fly'), children's game that also recalls extensive use of pigeons to carry military information in World War I. Red and blue are the colours of Paris, and the blue smocks recall the blue uniforms of French soldiers (as at line 275).

94–8   'At Bon Marche, Spring Outfits Available Now'. Bon Marché, large department store in the rue de Babylone, subject of Zola's 1883 novel, *Au Bonheur des Dames* (*Ladies' Paradise*) (Higonnet 200).

99   'jeunesse dorée', gilded youth, used of wealthy, spoilt young people, but also of the buds on the sycamore trees.

100–1   Mauve or purple is the ritual colour used in Lent.

103–4   'Crocuses, / Chionodoxa', flowers of early spring. Crocuses are frequently mauve. Blue or white chionodoxa, meaning 'glory of the snow', a suitable name for a fairy-tale princess. Serbia also recalls the assassination of the Archduke at Sarajevo that triggered World War I.

106–8   'chef d'oeuvre', masterpiece. The floral pageant runs from crocuses, to lily of the valley sold on 1 May (see lines 235–59) to the dog roses of early summer. The dog-roses reverse the gaze of painters (lines 21–2) by watching the annual pilgrimage of gypsies to Saintes-Marie-de-la-Mer in the Camargue on 23–5 May; 'wanes', an unusual spelling of 'wains', or wagons. 'Charles's wain', another name for the Great Bear (see line 445).

110–13   'Roses from Lyons', a major city, south-east of Paris. Unlike dog roses, they are 'scentless' (*fade*?), yet 'plastic', or moulded. In 1913 Joseph Pernet-Ducher named a hybrid tea-rose 'Mme Edouard Herriot' after the wife of the then mayor of Lyons.

114–15   The French painter J.A.D. Ingres (1780–1867) apparently did not paint Mme Nélie Jacquemart-André (1841–1912), herself a portrait painter and art collector. Her home became the Musée Jacquemart-André at 158, Blvd. Haussmann.

116–21   In February 1919, paintings stored underground for safety were rehung in the Louvre, including the fifteenth-century century *Pietà* from Villeneuve-lès-Avignon; Edouard Manet's controversial nude, *Olympia* (1863), first displayed in 1907 after a campaign by Georges Clemenceau (on Manet, see line 290); 'Gil[l]es', Watteau's painting of a Pierrot (1718–19); 'Mantegna's Seven Deadly Sins', properly *Minerva Chasing the Vices from the Garden of Virtue* (ca. 1502); J.-B.-S Chardin (1699–1779) specialised in domestic scenes and still life.

122–4   'Unetiolated', not pale from being stored in a dark, underground place. Shakespeare's Macbeth claims of his murdered victim, 'Duncan is in his grave. / After life's fitful fever, he sleeps well' (III.ii.22–3). The paintings implicitly contrast with dead soldiers, who cannot be resurrected, and may not 'sleep well'.

125–7   Greeted rapturously as 'Wilson le Juste' on his arrival in Paris for the peace talks, President Woodrow Wilson brought his fourteen-point plan, which promised more than it could deliver (MacMillan 3–20). 'Gargantua', figuring old Europe, was an anarchic giant, and title character of Rabelais' fantasy (1534–5); his urine was indeed 'diluvial', or flood-like (the French describe heavy rain as 'pluie diluvienne'). Wilson's 'innocent enjoyment' appeared to Clemenceau 'pathetic naiveté' (MacMillan 23).

128   'chrysalids', cocoons or pupae that will release butterflies (as the buds release leaves).

131   Easter (Good Friday, 18 April 1919)). 'Grand Guignol', ('blood and guts') was a violent, sensational type of melodrama performed at the Grand Guignol theatre in Montmartre (see lines 181–2).

133   Ritual self-flagellation was a regular feature of Good Friday processions.

135   Little Jesus does a pee-pee. 'Le petit jésus', pretty child, can also be slang for a boy prostitute.

136   Lilac flowers near the end of Lent, its colour echoing that of the church draperies (101, 155).

137–8   *Song of Solomon* 8.8: 'We have a little sister, and she has no breasts' (see also *Song of Soloman* 2.11–12 for its evocation of spring).

139–41   'Quality milk from the Rambouillet farm', the first of a series of street signs. Rambouillet, a small town south-west of Paris, where Louis XVI created the Ferme de Rambouillet, the Queen's dairy, for Marie-Antoinette. The Hôtel Rambouillet (in Paris) was the first and greatest French *salon* (see HM's novel *Madeleine*, chapter IX).

142–3   'The telephone directory can be consulted here'.

144–5   'Delicatessen, for best quality cold cuts'.

146–7   'Pre-meal drinks' / 'Food for diabetics' (literally, 'diabetic food').

148   'Your clothes dyed black in 24 hours' (literally, 'mourning in 24 hours'). This and the previous sign are examples of 'catachresis', the application of a term to something it does not properly denote. According to MacMillan (26–7), in the Paris of 1919 'almost every other woman wore mourning'.

149 'Gentlemen-and-ladies', written thus to reflect its pronunciation on the streets by waiters, etc. (see lines 157, 191–2).

150–4 A Roman temple to Mercury, the winged messenger of the gods, once stood on Montmartre, where the cathedral of the Sacré Coeur had recently been completed (dedicated October 1919). *Templum* is Latin for a sacred space, but 'Little temples' might refer to the circular kiosks on the boulevards or even open-air urinals (*pissoirs*).

153–4 Harpagon is *The Miser* of Molière's play (1668), who regards his money as his blood (see V.iii). East of the Sacré Coeur (sacred heart) is the rue de la Goutte d'Or (golden drop), its name derived from the wealth of the vineyards formerly on that site, so the 'golden drop of Harpagon's blood' (money) may be contrasted with the blood of the Sacred Heart. But if the 'golden drop' is urine (as at lines 127–8), this might refer to the homosexual activities for which the *pissoirs* had been notorious since the eighteenth century.

155–6 In a typical bar-tabac: vermouth is a type of aperitif; bocks are glasses of beer.

158–60 'Don't close the door, please, the Primus [a compressed air device] will take care of it.'

161 ouvriers: workmen, who discuss recent news items.

162 'the eight-hour day', demanded by the workers and voted on by the government on 17 and 23 April, but the difficulties of implementing it resulted in a general strike on 1 May (lines 235–59, 263; Hausser 723, 724).

163 Henri Landru was a serial killer. The police investigated his activities from April to May 1919.

164 According to a programme for 2 May 1919, the learned seal was 'Bichette' and her trainer was Capitaine Juge; the Nouveau Cirque was at 251, rue Saint-Honoré.

165 On 19 February, the anarchist Emile Cottin attempted to assassinate Georges Clemençeau, chairman of the Peace Conference (see notes on lines 35–9, 116–21; Hausser 715; MacMillan 150–1). Cottin was condemned to death in March, but reprieved. His name suggests that of the Abbé Charles Cotin (1604–82), habitué of the Hôtel Rambouillet (see *Madeleine*, 55).

166 Jacques Benigne Bossuet (1624–1704), bishop and preacher, famous for his funeral sermons, particularly that on Henrietta Maria, Charles I's queen ('chanting dead queens').

167–70 Four adjectives probably refer to the previous discussion: *méticuleux*, punctilious, scrupulous (Cottin?); *bélligerants*, aggressive, warlike (the Germans, according to the newspapers?); *hebdomadaire*, weekly (of the eight-hour day); *immonde*, monstrous, foul (Landru?).

171–4 The Roman Legions in their winged helmets could be seen as invaders of Gaul (France) (like the defeated Germans) or else as France's departing allies.

175–7 Père Lachaise, third of the trio of seventeenth-century clerics, was the Jesuit confessor of Louis XIV and gave his name to Paris's most famous cemetery. He appears wearing a curtain (introducing the theatre of war), embroidered with the letter H (pronounced 'ash' in French, and so suggesting the words of the English funeral service, 'Dust to dust, and ashes to ashes' – in French *hache* also means axe.

180   Henri Rousseau (1844–1910), known as the Douanier (customs officer) was a French 'Sunday' painter whose paintings ('beautiful and horrible') were admired by the avant-garde, especially after Picasso gave a famous dinner for him (1908). HM may have known his painting *La Guerre* (1894).

181–2   The artistic representation of violent events now dominates the poem. World War I failed conspicuously to conform to any rules, let alone the unities of time, place and action required of classical tragedy; it was closer to Grand Guignol (line 131), which left 'The stage . . . thick with corpses'.

183   *gaillards*, big, strapping fellows.

184   *eidola*, (Greek) ghosts, spirits, images.

186   Killed in action (literally, 'dead on the field of honour').

188–9   'The poor man!'

190   'petites bourgeoises', middle-class women, collecting money for war victims (lines 149, 157). Picardie is a province in northern France, site of much of the fighting in World War I.

194   ghoul-like, ghouls rob graves and eat corpses.

196–7   The battle of the Marne (1914) was the worst battle of World War I for the French in terms of losses, their army being almost cut off by German forces in eastern France. The river Marne flows westwards to join the Seine near Paris, where its banks were lined with 'guingettes', dance halls, popular at weekends.

198   'The Grand[s] Boulevards', a series of wide streets running north of the rue Saint-Honoré, on an east-west axis, lined with theatres and cinemas – a favourite Sunday afternoon walk (the poem seems to zig-zag east from Concorde to the Louvre, west along the rue Saint-Honoré towards the Madeleine, then east along the Grands Boulevards). From here to line 234 is a description of the Grands Boulevards.

200–3   'Cloacae' (Latin), sewers below the boulevards; 'Hot indiarubber', from car tyres – by 1914, there were 25,000 cars in Paris (Higonnet 187); 'Poudre de riz', face powder; 'Algerian tobacco' (see line 434) was cheap – themes of empire and racial alterity re-appear, picking up on 'Zig-Zag' (line 3), cigarette papers rolled around Algerian tobacco and joints.

204–5   'Monsieur Jourdain', *Le Bourgeois Gentilhomme* of Molière's play (1670), dresses up and joins in a Turkish dance in order to become a 'Mamamouchi'. He is here pictured in the blue and red uniform of the French Algerian army, the Zouaves. '[P]remier danseur', chief soloist; 'Ballet Turque' [turc], Turkish ballet.

206   'Dat's good!', the slogan advertising the breakfast food, 'Banania', on a famous poster showing a Senegalese rifleman sitting under a palm tree.

208   'YANKEES', Americans, either in Paris for the Peace Conference, or

staying on after World War I. African-Americans often settled in Montmartre, where they found a tolerant atmosphere (Higonnet 340–2). '[A]nd say besides...', Shakespeare's Moor of Venice, Othello, just before his suicide, remembers how he summarily executed a Turk who had 'Beat a Venetian, and traduced the State' (V.ii. 354 – thus picking up the Turkish theme).

209–10 *Mardi gras*, Shrove Tuesday, the last day before Lent, the period of forty days fasting before Easter; *Carême Prenant,* Shrovetide, the days before the start of Lent, a period of merry-making or 'Carnival', before the fast; here linked with the Peace Conference, as a celebration before repentance and deprivation.

211–13 Crêpes (Shrovetide pancakes) become 'crape' thin black mourning veils; *Cho-co-lat*, Cho-co-late – the second 'o' is long, and emphasised in French pronunciation.

214 'The women rock themselves backwards and forwards on their haunches.'

216 Square-cut beards, as portrayed on Assyrian statues.

218 Tart: sharp, acid; 'The tart little race' might be the Armenians, victims of Turkish massacres, who sent a special delegation to the Peace Conference (MacMillan 377).

220–1 'Yesyesyes, isn't it exciting – and such good value for money. Cheese isn't a rational dish' (see line 37).

222–4 'A-a-ah yes, he's a charming boy. / I think every honest woman must recognise herself in Anna Karenina' – Tolstoy's novel *Anna Karenina* (1877) is the story of a woman who abandons marriage and child for her lover (see line 282).

225 'catalepsy': a seizure or trance in which consciousness is suspended (for other tranced moments, see lines 20, 320). French café gossip is contrasted with the silence of Germans.

226–31 Subaqueous: (constructed) under water; this passage echoes the preface to *Madeleine*, where 'Life' (or as here, 'Experience') is the material out of which Art is gradually formed.

233–4 With these lines, the description of the Grands Boulevards comes to an end, suggesting, perhaps, that the life of the Boulevards provides raw material needing to be formed into speech or words, if it is to become art ('coming to' could mean coming back to consciousness). Lines 232–4 themselves burst into 'vastness' after the six narrow lines that precede them (see also Tennyson's poem, 'Vastness').

235–50 1 May is celebrated as Labour Day in France, but in 1919 there was a general strike in Paris, with violent clashes between the authorities and the workers, some of whom marched with knives between their teeth (Hausser 726; MacMillan 273). The vertical lettering emphasises the disruption of normal order, representing the lines of marchers, and possibly the stems of the (absent) lily of the valley, usually sold on 1 May, to give to friends or sweethearts as bringer of luck (line 106).

260–2 The struggle between the chaos of life and the structure of art (lines

226–32) now becomes a 'ritual fight' between two virgins, as the year progresses from 'The wicked April moon' (*la lune rousse*) to the month of May, sacred to the Virgin Mary. The April moon is the lunar month after Easter, characterised by cold, harsh winds that seem to scorch (*roussir*) the new growth. '[H]er sweet body' could be that of Paris.

263   Punning on the English expression, 'the silence of the grave', *la grève* is the strike (on 1 May), with a further underlying wordplay, since *la grève* means the river bank – the place de *Grève* (now, place de l'Hôtel de Ville) being where Parisian workers assembled to *faire la grève*, or go on strike.

268   'the mysterious island gardens' seem to be those of the Carrousel, running from the Arc de Triomphe du Carrousel down to the Tuileries.

269–71   The Seine winds westwards through the centre of Paris reaching the sea at Le Havre. 'Ruminating', literally, chewing the cud, and thus recycling or recirculating, also suggests the river's passage through the fertile dairy-farming province of Normandy. Initially associated with the underworld (line 10), the Seine is here (and later, line 414) associated with the Freudian unconscious, which increasingly asserts itself as dreams (line 271, and see lines 310, 376), anticipated by the melting of the Louvre (line 265; compare lines 311–15).

272   'King-fishers', small, bright blue diving birds.

273–4   Paris now becomes a sequence of pictures: the 'two-dimensional' (as at line 403) silhouette of the Eiffel Tower (a favourite subject for artists) is 'etched' (engraved, black on white), while the soldiers encamped in the Tuileries are drawn in coloured chalk, and the page ends with (imaginary) oil paintings.

275–9   'The *Poilus*' (literally 'hairy'), French World War I soldiers in blue uniforms, with *Tierre de Sienne* (burnt Sienna, reddish brown) packs, around the 'gray sphinx' look like the chalk sketches, 'edited' (i.e., published) in the rue des Pyramides, a street where souvenirs are sold. The combination of sphinx and pyramids recalls Napoleon's campaign in Egypt, as well as World War I operations in Egypt (MacMillan 382–3, 401).

280–5   'Désœuvrement' (idleness, lack of occupation, suffered by demobilised soldiers) suggests Vronsky; 'Apprehension' suggests Anna, the lovers at the centre of Tolstoy's *Anna Karenina* (line 224). In part 4, they wake from similar dreams of a sinister Russian peasant (a 'mujik'), perhaps unconsciously anticipating the Bolshevik Revolution (1917).

286–9   Even the most violent and calamitous moments of history can be transformed into the tranquillity of art. Clio, the Greek muse of history, becomes a French painter, stilling the watery flux of life. Shadrach et al. were cast by Nebuchadnezzar into the fiery furnace (Daniel 3.12–30), but in art they become 'motionless and plastic'.

290–3   'Manet's *Massacres*. . . ' a series of paintings imagined as hanging in the Louvre, depicting violent moments of French history: Manet (1832–83) is imagined portraying the massacres of 'les journées de Juin' (days of June 1848 when protesters were rounded up, disarmed, and killed by the army); David (1748–1825), as painting the taking of the Bastille (14 July 1789, the beginning of the French Revolution); while Nicolas Poussin (1594–1665), as depicting the uprisings of the Fronde (1649, 1652) (see *Madeleine*, 11–12). Pages 13–15 of the Hogarth edition survive in a proof, corrected by HM. Here the first imaginary painting was originally 'Cézanne's *Quatorze Juillet*' – apparently altered because its subject, '14 July', was too close to David's. 'Manet's *Massacres des Jours de Juin*' was substituted. Manet actually painted *The Execution of Maximilian* (1867) and the executions of May 1871. HM's revisions produce a historical sequence, running from the strike of 1 May 1919, back through the risings of 1848, 1789 and 1652, to illustrate French political resistance.

294–5 Like Clio (but not like Vronsky), the Virgin has been busy – creating business for (and later actually window-dressing) Paris's three largest and best-known department stores – les Galéries Lafayette, le Bon Marché (see line 95), and la Samaritaine.

295–7 According to HM's notes to *Paris*, during Lent, department store windows displayed wax models dressed for First Communion in white veils and ties (knots of ribbon) as 'bait', to encourage young girls to participate by showing the pretty clothes they could wear. But these 'Waxen Pandoras' are also 'bait' in a further sense, since (according to Hesiod, lines 80–82) Pandora was sent by Zeus to tempt Prometheus and punish him from stealing fire from the gods. Pandora was modelled from clay (not wax), and carried a jar containing all the evils of the world. When she opened it, they all flew out into the world, except Hope (HM's own name), left inside the jar.

298 *Catéchisme de Persévérance*, a popular nineteenth-century Catholic manual by Jean-Joseph Gaume. The decrees of the 'Seven Œcumenical Councils' (Nicea I, AD 325–Nicea II, AD 787) embody the central doctrines of Christianity; 'format' means 'size'; *Bibliotheque Rose*, a series of books for girls published by Hachette.

301–2 'First communion'. Prometheus has swallowed the 'bait' of Pandora, or the communion wafer, or is excited by the First Communicants.

303–5 'Petits Lycéens', little high-school children. 'Por-no-gra-phie', spelled out as if for children, is a Greek word meaning, literally, writings about prostitution; 'pigmy brides' are miniature brides of Christ. 'Pigmy' is a Greek word for the forearm or fist, anticipating the cannibal imagery that follows ('teknophagiai', the eating of children, is discussed by JH in *Themis* 248–9).

306–7 'Little St. Hugh' (not an actual saint), according to anti-Semitic legend, a child murdered by Jews in Lincoln (1255). Chaucer's *Prioress's Tale* tells a similar story. By eating the body of Christ (the Jew) at first communion, the children 'avenge' St. Hugh's murder.

308 A photographic studio in Paris? A peepshow?

312 Périgord is a rural region in south-western France, part of the poem's tour of provinces.

310–15 The Louvre is the great palace at the heart of Paris, now an art gallery; the Ritz is a hotel at 15, Place Vendôme; the Palais-Royal[e] is opposite the Louvre; the Hôtel de Ville, the Paris Mairie (or town hall), is east of the Louvre on the rue de Rivoli. All are solid, indeed massive buildings, that could only appear 'light and frail' in a rising atmosphere of dreams (see line 265).

316–17 'junketing', feasting, merrymaking. Masks and dominoes are carnival disguises (the domino is the cloak to go with the mask), typically worn by the aristocracy, but here by 'citizens', thus anticipating the Revolution.

318 'On the occasion of the marriage of Monsieur le Dauphin', the marriage celebrations of the future Louis XVI to Marie-Antoinette. In the course of these (30–31 May 1770) a display of fireworks created a stampede in which several hundred people were crushed to death or pushed into the river.

319–21 The Hôtel de l'Elysée, 3, rue de Beaune, where HM stayed in Paris and apparently wrote this poem, was a hotel in the modern sense, as well as in the older sense of a grand town house, formerly the property of Mme du Deffand, famous for her *salon*. 'Tranced' (line 20, and perhaps line 45), trance states, and the automatic writing they generated, were to fascinate the Surrealists. It is possible that the whole poem, flickering between 'real' and imagined Paris sights, was generated by this 'tranced' moment of gazing out of the window (Keatsian 'magic casements, opening on the foam / Of perilous seas, in fairy lands forlorn').

322 'Hawkers . . . liturgically', street peddlars . . . in the style of a church service.

323–4 'Triptolemos', a legendary king of Eleusis who founded the Mysteries and taught men agriculture (including how to make bread). As a baby (wrapped in swaddling clothes that make him 'loaf-shaped'), he was loved by Demeter (Ceres), probably identified with the 'women in black shawls'.

325–6 'Workmen in pale blue', wearing denim overalls; 'Barrows' belong to street vendors displaying their wares.

332 Ovid, Roman poet and storyteller (43 BC–AD 17), was exiled to Tomis on the Black Sea, but not a 'thrall' (i.e., slave) in Fairyland (as was the narrator of Keats's poem, 'La Belle Dame Sans Merci'). The resulting 'lost romance' is imagined as having inspired Italian painters, as their 'guild-secret', peculiar to their craft.

339–40 Three landmarks of seventeenth-century Paris to the north and east, by 1919 in a state of disrepair, and thus 'exquisitely dying' (see line 41).

342–5 Quiet was expected for the dying. The eight bars of music are marked 'dim—in—u-en-do' (growing softer) to 'ppp', pianissimo, very quiet indeed. The melancholy aria is 'Lascia ch'io pianga', from Handel's opera *Rinaldo* (1711), 'Let me weep for my cruel fate, and let me sigh for my liberty' (recalling Ovid's misery in exile?).

346–7 The beautiful church of Saint Thomas d'Aquin (begun 1688, completed in 1766) stands near the end of the rue de Beaune. L'impasse des Deux Anges, (the blind alley of the two angels), is close by. The angels may be linked with Jacob (see Genesis 28.12, or 32.24–9), though 'two angels' are particularly connected with Lot and the destruction of the cities of the plain (Genesis 19.1–17), punished by God for homosexuality (see Cocteau, 28–9, 47; 45, 66). The name of the 'impasse' might also suggest lesbianism. It was close to Natalie Barney's house (at 20, rue Jacob) and is referred to in Djuna Barnes's *The Ladies' Almanack* (1928).

347–9 'Impasse', a blind alley, also suggests 'deadlock' (both in French and English), and 'impassive' (i.e., blank or inexpressive, *impassible*). The French expression for walls without windows, *murs aveugles* (blind walls) may have suggested the comparison with blind dogs. The ghosts, watched by the 'impassive windows' (compare line 108), introduce a pageant of the city's famous dead.

353 Sebastopol, port on the Black Sea, besieged and eventually captured (1856) by English and French troops (greatly aided by Algerians, the 'Zouaves') during the Crimean War, and commemorated by a street name and a métro station.

354–61 The memorial plaque for the playwright (1622–73) on his house at 40, rue de Richelieu, on the Right Bank, north of the Louvre (see lines 153, 204). 'The dying seventeenth century' is followed by the memorial plaque for the Enlightenment philosopher, Voltaire (1694–1778), who died at no.1, rue de Beaune, next door to or even part of HM's hotel.

362–5 Chateaubriand, Romantic poet and memoirist (1768–1848), died close by, at 118–20 rue du Bac, with the blind Mme Récamier at his bedside (lines 64–5). These writers typify three different centuries, and three different French styles.

367–8 'Paradise' is almost an anagram of 'Paris' and 'dies'. Les Champs Elysées, Paris's most famous avenue, means 'the Elysian fields', in classical literature, the home of the dead.

369 The French critic Charles Saint-Beuve (1804–69) was the friend and rival of the poet and novelist Victor Hugo (1802–85), and the lover of his wife Adèle. The Pont Neuf ('New Bridge', now the oldest, completed 1604) would take Saint-Beuve from his house on the Left Bank to the Right (where the Hugos lived, at 6 place des Vosges).

370–3 The duc de la Rochefoucauld (1613–80), author of *Maximes* (1664) and a close friend of Mme de Lafayette (1634–93), author of *La Princesse de Clèves* (1678). He passes Saint-Beuve on the Pont Neuf as he crosses to the Left Bank to visit Mme Lafayette in the rue Ferou. They cannot see each other, perhaps because of the centuries between them, but the duc had figured in Saint-Beuve's great study of the seventeenth century, *Port-Royal* (1840–59). The *salon d'automne* exhibited avant-garde painting; it was originally formed by a group of Fauvists and Post-Impressionists in 1903 (Shattuck 61).

375   'It's close, sultry' (literally, heavy, as in 'Heavy sweet going', line 311).
377   'Benediction', a Catholic service. 'Notre-Dame-des-Champs' (Our Lady of the fields) is one of the oldest churches in Paris; formerly standing in fields on Montparnasse, it was rebuilt in 1876. Its métro station is south of rue du Bac on the Nord-Sud line, between Port-Royal (line 439) and the garden of the nuns of St. Vincent de Paul, on the rue de Babylone (now the Jardin Catherine Laboure).
379–82   The Virgin wears the elaborately starched headdress of the nuns of St. Vincent de Paul (winged like the Roman helmets of line 172) and probably sits in their convent garden (see above), where the west wall would have been covered with plum and apricot trees, and there are still box hedges. The Holy Ghost descended as a dove, and 'cooing' and '(dove)-cots' are common to babies and doves (compare Cocteau 22: 'Dieu roucoule au sommet des arbres').
383   'The Seven Stages', possibly half of the fourteen Stations of the Cross, performed on Good Friday, representing Christ's final sufferings; 'cut in box', either means carved in boxwood, or from topiary (pruning box hedges into shapes). Churches display branches of box during Easter week.
384–6   White ('Madonna') lilies, the Virgin's flower. Votive offerings result from a religious promise. The Jap(anese) convert is the painter L.T. Foujita (1886–1968), who painted pictures of the Virgin and Child in soft colours (1917–18), often in shapes resembling bulbs.
387–9   'troubadour', Provençal travelling minstrel. The cult of courtly love voiced in troubadour poetry was linked with the cult of the Virgin; 'her', i.e., to her. 'Venial sins' are lesser ones than Deadly Sins (at lines 120, 426–7).
390–1   The garden wall becomes the evening sky, hung with the plums of Paradise, where wasps never fret (eat away) the fruit; on the Solférino bridge, however, people look like flies, nibbling into the apricot (coloured) sky (lines 399–401).
392–3; 396   'Freedom!' 'The Press!' names of evening newspapers shouted by street vendors.
394–5   'Petit-Palais', built for the 1900 World Exhibition, west of the Place de Concorde, and perhaps just visible from a high west-facing window at the end of the rue de Beaune. At sunset in the Algerian desert the 'muezzin' gives the Muslim call to prayer.
400–4   'Fiacres', light, horse-drawn four-wheeled cabs. Looking westward, HM might just have seen figures on the old Pont Solférino (demolished 1961), silhouetted like flies against the celestial (heavenly) evening haze; 'tippetted pelisse', a fur-collared cloak. Louis-Philippe, 'the citizen king', reigned 1830–48, when portraits in silhouette, cut from black paper, were in vogue.
405–6   The Quais are the streets along the banks of the Seine, where the 'bouquinistes' (box-owners, booksellers) sell their wares from green

boxes, which they lock up at night.
407   Paris has twenty *arrondissements* (administrative districts). The VIIme lies immediately south of the river, on the Left Bank, and includes the rue de Beaune; like the neighbouring VIme, this was an up-market address, known as the 'Faubourg Saint-Germain'.
410   'Hyperbórean', northern. The poem prepares to move up to Montmartre, in the north of Paris.
413   'Ramparts', mounds built for defence. The Louvre was initially built as a fortress (in 1200). Here ramparts keep the river, and perhaps the unconscious, at bay.
414–15   Sigmund Freud (1856–1939), Viennese theorist of sexuality and the unconscious, dredges the river, associated with rising dreams (1ines 269–72). The combination of Freud and electricity evokes modern life. Paris had had electrically lit advertisements from 1912 (Higonnet 145, 358, and compare 'Contrastes': 'Il pleut les globes electriques', Blaise Cendrars, *Poésies Complètes*, ed. Claude Leroy [Paris: Denoël, 2001], p. 71).
416–18   Taxis line up on the page, as they do on the streets.
421   'their meat', perhaps their clients (see line 4; the opening themes are now replayed).
422   'padre', 'Father' (a Catholic priest) strikes at the Moulin Rouge (literally, the Red Windmill), Paris's most famous cabaret show (on the Place Blanche, Montmartre). To tilt with windmills is to make an ineffectual attack (from *Don Quixote*).
423   Black music notes become African-American musicians playing jazz; 'syncopation', shifting of the regular musical beat, as in jazz. Today this sentence is disturbingly racist, although the black musicians, like the lesbians in the following lines, introduce a liberating discourse of racial and sexual alterity. Jazz was brought to Paris by black US army bands at the end of World War I, and was fashionable in Montmartre (Higonnet 341).
425, 430   Literally, all the cards (or maps) work with, walk with or go out with a match, but the exact meaning is hard to decide. It might refer to packs of cards given out in cafés, with boxes of matches, but 'cartes' was also slang for prostitutes, and an 'allumette' might be a sexual tease, or even a penis. A song refrain?
426   Fifty pairs of glasses, designed to correct American 'astigmatism' (a sight defect that prevents focusing), reflect a (leg) show, saucily entitled 'the Masque of the Seven Deadly Sins' (see line 120), a pseudo-religious title for a secular event, perhaps suggesting a further clash between the Virgin and 'The wicked April moon'.
428–9   Stage performers, like courtesans, were often supposed lesbian, and lesbianism was fashionable in Paris at this time (Higonnet 112–13). The spelling 'gurls' may indicate an American accent, but 'girls' was also French slang both for lesbians and chorus girls.
431   Dawn brings the poem's time scheme of a single day to a close.

432 Paul Verlaine (1844–96), lyric poet and decadent, fell in love with the precocious Arthur Rimbaud (1854–91), author of 'L'Alchimie du verbe' (a section of his prose poem *Une Saison en Enfer*). 'Alchemy', the transformation of base metals into gold, is also a figure for the coming of dawn. 'Absynthe' [unusually spelled with a 'y'] is a powerful green spirit distilled from wormwood to which Verlaine was addicted. Picasso's 1903 painting, *Portrait du poète Cornuti, ou l'Absinthe* is a form of homage to Verlaine. Algerian tobacco was used to roll cheap cigarettes and joints (lines 3, 203).

437–8 Raymond Poincaré was president of France (1913–20). The poem here rocks between homosexuality and heterosexuality (the marriage bed, birth), between couples and single lives.

439 'Port-Royal', maternity hospital on the Left Bank, formerly a convent associated with Jansenism, a movement within the French seventeenth-century church persecuted by the authorities (and the focus of Saint-Beuve's study, *Port-Royal*). In chapter XVI of *Madeleine*, Madeleine visits the Abbaye, whose mistress, Mère Agnès Arnauld, is a portrait of JH (157).

440 This line suggests Duncan Grant's painting *Le Crime et le Châtiment* (ca. 1909), especially since Dostoevsky's novel (1866) was usually translated *Crime et Châtiment*. HM knew Grant, and may have known that the painting showed Marjorie Strachey reading that novel.

442 'Les Halles', until the late 1960s, Paris's main food market, rebuilt of wrought iron and glass (1866).

444 'I salute you Paris full of grace', echoing the Catholic prayer 'Ave Maria', 'Je vous salue Marie pleine de grace' (see Dedication; Cocteau 82: 'Je vous salue pleine de grace. . . o sainte mère').

445 The poem ends with the constellation of Ursa Major, the great she-bear, part of the private code between HM and JH, who sometimes signed off letters to HM with this star sign in reverse.

448 The original Hogarth Press edition mistakenly printed the poem's completion date as '1916'; Virginia Woolf hand corrected most of the copies by writing '9' over the '6'.

On the final page, HM makes a further highly original gesture by providing a set of notes to her admittedly difficult poem. Though not without precedent (Pope had annotated his 'Dunciad'), it was unusual for an author to annotate her own text thus. Brief and fragmentary though her notes are, they offer a fresh perspective on the poem, and incidentally anticipate T. S. Eliot's use of notes in *The Waste Land* (1922).

Addendum
Sandeep Parmar

HM made six substantive changes to *Paris* for its republication in the *Virginia Woolf Quarterly* in 1973.
The following lines were omitted: 131–5; 294–7 and 302–7.
352   'Masses' was replaced by 'dirges'.
379–91   These thirteen lines, commencing 'The Virgin...' and ending with '...of Paradise', were omitted and replaced by the following fourteen lines:

> The Virgin sits in her garden;
> She wears the blue habit and the
> white head-dress of the nuns of
>   St. Vincent of Paul.
> The fourteen stations of the Cross are
> carved in box;
> Lilies bloom, blue, green and pink,
> The bulbs were votive offerings
> From a converted Japanese. An angelic troubadour
> Sings her songs of her Son's courtly love.
> Upon the wall of sunset sky wasps never fret
> The plums of Paradise.
>
> Upon the wall of sunset-sky wasps never fret
>   The plums of Paradise.
>
>   [*La Liberté La Presse!*, etc]

423   'Niggers' was replaced by the more acceptable term 'Negroes'.

Notes on the Poems and Essays

Moods and Tensions

Mothers   'Mater Saeva Cupidinum' is the title of Horace's *Ode* XIX, Book I. It could be translated as 'wild mother of the passions'. The line 'Trying to stamp it with love's brittle seal' appears as 'With love's false heraldry stamping the real' in *M&T* and as 'Turning life into something stylized and unreal' in *Poems*. 'Logaoedic' here describes Aeschylus's verse as being a mix of dactyls and trochees.

The Copper-Beech in St. Giles' Churchyard   The poem has been assigned the composition date of July 1961. HM notes in *M&T* that 'Have ye not seen us walking every day?' is from *On the Death of Mr. William Hervey* by Abraham Cowley. She also points out that the word 'Mass' is pronounced with a long *a* by English Catholics. A manuscript version of this poem confirms that it was completed in July 1961 at the Randolph Hotel, which still stands, in Oxford.

The Death of Cats and Roses   HM notes 'Maart is the Afrikaans for March. My cat came to me in that month, hence his name.' A notebook draft of this poem bears the dedication 'For J.P.'

Et in Arcadia Ego   HM notes in *M&T76*: 'Et in Arcadia Ego is the inscription on a Roman tomb, known only from its depiction in paintings, of which the most famous is by Poussin. There is a division of opinion as to whether the speaker is the dead man or the tomb itself. In the first case, the meaning would be "I too have had my happiness"; in the second: "Death reigns even in Arcadia". I am indebted for this information to the kindness of Miss Mary Lascelles. In my poem the two interpretations are used as variations on the same theme.' In the manuscript copy sent to Mary Lascelles, HM explains her reference in line 6 of the poem: 'The large insects which in hot countries swarm at dusk and shed their dirty-yellow incandescent wings are popularly known in South Africa as "flying ants".' She also notes, after 'Tityrus, and Amaryllis sleep': 'This is meant to be a quantitative (is there such a word?) line, and to be heavily stressed (like schoolboys scanning their hexameters!) [. . .].' After 'Of sodden, trodden, frostnipped willow leaves' she has written: 'I can't find the willow as the emblem of the forlorn lover in either Theocritus or the *Eclogues*. Perhaps it occurs in the post-classical pastorals? In any case unhappy love is the burden of the songs of Virgil's shepherd.'

The Land of Uz   The epigraph is taken from opening lines of the Book of Job.

The Legend of the Painted Room   'The Painted Room' is part of an old tavern that is now the Golden Cross, a shopping centre and restaurant in Cornmarket Street (Oxford). The original site dates from the late twelfth century, and Shakespeare is said to have stayed at the inn there. The walls of the room, which have been preserved, are painted to look like tapestry. In correspondence, HM vaguely suggests to Mary Lascelles that the second line of the poem originates in something by Seneca – but she cannot recall the source exactly. It seems fitting that Hope, whose poetry and novels relied heavily on historical research, claims Clio the muse of history as her own. HM visited the room with Valerie Eliot, and this is mentioned in the poem: 'The wife of a great poet lately dead, / (A poet who had long endured / A semi-mystical, Arthurian wound / From an Archangel's spear, which she had cured)'. '*Il miglior fabbro*' is from Eliot's dedication of *The Waste Land* to Ezra Pound. It could be translated as 'the better craftsman'.

'Une Maison Commode, Propre, et Belle...'   The poem is based on a sonnet by Christophe Plantin's (1514–89), 'The Happiness of this World'. HM's title is taken from Plantin's first line, which is 'To have a house that is commodious, clean and beautiful'.

The Rendez-Vous   'Quaerens me sedisti lassus', a line from *Dies Irae*, used as part of the Roman Catholic Requiem Mass, could be translated as 'Faint and weary thou has sought me'. The scene references the Biblical story of the Samarian woman in the Gospel of John. 'Sub specie aeternitatis' could be translated as 'under the aspect of eternity'. HM offers these notes: 'I do not think that the scene has been painted by Rembrandt, and it is certainly not the subject of a Ravenna mosaic. What I mean is that it lends itself equally well to be depicted realistically or symbolically.' A letter to HM from Mary Lascelles (18 February 1976?) states: 'You say, in a note, that you are doubtful whether Rembrandt painted that subject – the woman of Samaria. I am not sure about the painting, but there are at least two drawings: one, the more tremendous, in Birmingham; the other, a slight sketch, in the Ashmolean [Oxford]. I expect your memory held the impression, and then you distrusted it, as one so often does, in dejection.' HM points out that Sychar is 'near where St John places the episode [and] is probably the vanished village of Sychāra.' HM writes in her notebook about this poem: 'The reality of which the meeting of Jacob and Rebecca at the *same* well was the foreshadowing. And this implied that the greatest and most momentous love-stories are merely symbols, shadows of the great reality, i.e. Christ's rendez-vous with *any* (however insignificant) human soul. My meeting at the well was at the Berthe Morisot exhibition. The actors in my drama were Charlotte Falre-Luce, Maria [Blanchard], Berthe Morisot and me. One of the purposes of BM's painting was that this might happen.' A notebook draft bears the dedication 'In the memory of M.B.'. It is very likely that 'M.B.' is HM's friend the Spanish painter Maria Blanchard, whom she met in Paris through a friend of Roger Fry, Angela Lavelli.

Bertha frightens Miss Bates   The poem's allusions are to characters in Jane Austen's novel *Emma*, with the exception of Bertha the 'maiden fair'. This character is taken from John Keats's unfinished poem 'The Eve of St Mark'. HM may have found a draft of the poem in a letter from Keats to his brother George dated September 1819. Bertha, Keats's heroine, is the same as that of Chatterton's in *Aella, a Tragic Interlude* (1777). The poem also references the superstition that the ghosts of 'those who are doomed within the year to die' can be seen on St Mark's Eve. HM's only note for the poem is about her usage of the word 'dustbin': 'I am told by an authority on the period that *dustbin* is an anachronism; but I do not see my way to dispensing with it.' After the line 'Would have no further need of lover, leech, or priest', HM notes: 'I read somewhere that Jane Austen told her family that Jane Fairfax did not live long. So I am supposing that she had a hemorrhage and died before her wedding day.' She adds: 'N.B. As to the 18th c. books I was thinking a little of Butler's *Analogy* (which perhaps she hadn't read?) but specially of the *very* unmystical sermons.'

In a Pagan Wood   '. . .I feel afraid, / As did the Greeks at high noon in a forest glade' alludes to Theocritus's *The Death of Daphnis*. HM removed this note in her proof copy of *M&T*. It originally read: 'Cf. Theocritus I. 15: It is not lawful for us to pipe at noon – we fear Pan.' Grinling Gibbons (1648–1721) was a renowned Dutch-born wood carver. 'Ενφημε ω χρη' could be translated as 'it is necessary to use words of good omen'.

Sickness and Recovery at the Cape of Good Hope in Spring   In the *Poems* version, line 13 reads 'And where in time and space save *now* and *here*'. HM changed 'now and here' to 'in the Cape' in *M&T*, thereby reflecting her later residence in England. HM notes in *M&T*76: '1. The bottle-brush is a type of myrtle. It has earned its nickname from the sprays of brilliant golden blossom, which, in shape, might suggest bottle-brushes to a prosaic mind. 2. *Braak* is the Afrikaans for fallow. 3. *Lente* is Afrikaans for spring. 4. The fields where the cattle graze in spring are white with arum lilies, which are as common in South Africa as dandelions in England; and the lily-like egrets sit on the backs of the cattle eating their ticks. 5. It is only for a short time at the beginning of spring that the doves sing what sounds to me "Say it with flow'rs." Later the song changes (at least to my ears) to "Cook with an Agar." 6. *Meises* is Afrikaans for lassies. 7. *Vygies* (pronounced *fachees*) is the local name at the Cape for mesembryanthemums. 8. The O.K. Bazaars are a chain of cheap stores with branches all over the Republic. They are much patronised by the Africans and "Coloured". 9. "Overseas", meaning Europe in general and England in particular, has taken the place of the Colonial term "Home".' 'Sursum Corda' is part of the Eucharist Prayer, which can be translated as 'Lift up your hearts'. For additional information about the poem's composition see note to 'Crossed in Love', p. 133.

Winter Trees   Earlier titles of this poem appear to have been 'Japan and Trees', 'Japanned Trees' or, later, 'A Vision of Winter Trees from my

Bedroom Window'. *M&T76* notes: '1. There is a carving in the Toshugo Shrine at Nikko of a kitten among peonies. It illustrates the following Zen question and answer. "What about a sleeping kitten under peonies in bloom?" "I would have nothing to do with it." 2. In the Boston Museum of Fine Arts there is a fifteenth-century Japanese ink-painting described as "A Buddhist Mystic laughing at the Moon."' HM adds elsewhere: 'Though I imply that the moon's phases were the cause of their laughter, I suspect that they may partly have been laughing at Shinto animism.'

A Portrait of the Second Eve, Painted in Pompeian Red   HM visited the Villa dei Misteri (Villa of the Mysteries) and its frescoed initiation chamber in September 1965. A large scrapbook of this tour, in HM's archive, consists mostly of postcards and handwritten notes documenting her impressions. Under a photograph postcard of the fresco 'The Frightened Lady' HM has written 'The initiated matron is now dancing as a Maenad'. 'The Frightened Lady' was an earlier title for this poem and presumably the poem's point of inspiration, as indicated by the epigraph. Drafts and notes reveal that HM compares the initiation of a Bacchante, depicted by the chamber's frescoes, with the Annunciation of the Virgin Mary and the temptation of Eve. An interesting comparison could be made between this poem's pagan origin and HM's poem about Donnatello's Annunciation scene in 'A Meditation on Donatello's Annunciation in the Church of Santa Croce, Florence'.

Amor Fati   An earlier title for this poem, in a notebook handwritten contents page for *M&T*, is 'Horoscope'. HM discusses consulting her 'stars' in her notebooks from 1956–7. It appears that, in doing so, she was seeking guidance about a relationship in which the boundaries of friendship and love had become blurred. It is worth noting that while there is some resonance here of Hope and Jane Harrison's private signature, the constellation Ursa Major, this poem is unlikely to be about her relationship with Harrison.

Heaven is Not Fairyland   HM notes that 'Pure act' is St Thomas Aquinas's definition of God.

A Meditation on Donatello's Annunciation in the Church of Santa Croce, Florence   During September 1959, HM and her sister Margot motored through Italy (from Milan to Rome) and stayed for ten days in Florence. HM read art history books on Renaissance Italian painters by Bernard Berenson, whom she had known during her youth. In a letter from HM to Jessie Stewart about her Italian trip, she writes a 'little memoir of Jane' is beginning to 'form up in my mind'. The poem makes reference to two sections of Dante Aligheri's *Divine Comedy: Purgatorio*, Canto XI, line 10 ('For of their will Angels make sacrifice / To God, singing *Hosanna*' in Part II, lines 38–9) and *Purgatorio*, Canto X, lines 29–45, paraphrased in Part II lines 42–50. HM notes elsewhere that her aunt, Georgina Grace Moncrieff, had written *Lyrical Meditations on the Paradiso* (Edinburgh, Moray Press, 1952). Moncrieff considers her book, a record of her personal reactions to the *Paradiso*, a 'broken reflection'. While *Lyrical*

Meditations isn't a paraphrase of Dante's *Paradiso*, it doesn't veer significantly from the original narrative. Hope's allusions to Dante's *Purgatorio* in this poem are of a very different vein. The historical personage Lucrezia Borgia (1480–1519), wife of Alfonse d'Este, Duke of Ferrara, serves as a figure of scandal and sin. 'Adeste' quite possibly means to evoke the religious hymn 'Adeste Fideles' ('O Come All Ye Faithful' in English). Adeste is the imperative – hence Mirrlees's line 'Yours is a *bidding* name' at the end of Part I [my italics].

Jesus Wept HM dictated this poem aloud to Margaret Ellis, who sent it to Robin Waterfield for *M&T76*. It was the last poem to be added to the manuscript.

Previously Unpublished Poems and Translations

I'd like to get into your dreams Manuscript, ca. late 1950s.

Crossed in Love Manuscript, ca. late 1950s. This poem seems to be based on a love affair with an unknown person that took place around 1957–9. HM notebooks from 1957 about this episode read: 'If I just shut the door, then the whole episode will have been pointless, i.e. it will be neither my meeting with my twin-soul; *or* my cross. [. . .] This affair with its hopes, disappointments and great misery has increased my faith. It is so exquisitely adapted to my spiritual needs. Hope from the beginning – but gradual realisation that the hope can only be fulfilled by keeping close to Our Lord and by waging the Christian warfare – practising justices self control reasonableness – all the things which I find so difficult.' Later on that year, she continues: 'Since writing above there has been my illness convalescence, and it has been sublimated into *Crossed in Love*. Well, yesterday I suddenly got scruples about *Sickness and Recovery* viz that it was too pagan and hence a sort of betrayal. I prayed but I was very upset and worried. Then, tho' it was Sunday, I thought (as I had missed mass) that I had better say my daily decade. It happened to be the turn of the first Glorious Mystery. And as I said it I realised that I had missed the real point of my material – Death and *Recovery* as the Spring Festival and *Easter*. It was what I need for Part II of the poem, the part about my recovery being too short and insignificant. It also solved my spiritual problem by showing quite clearly that the paganism was merely a sort of joke. Our Lord and Our Lady had helped me.' The poem's dedicatee 'V.E.' may be HM's friend Valerie Eliot, in whom she may have confided. 'Leucadian crag' refers to the suicide of the poet Sappho, who, according to legend, threw herself from a cliff after a failed love affair.

Love Lies Dying ca. 1973. The only version of this poem is in a manuscript found in a notebook among handwritten drafts of 'A Portrait of the Second Eve painted in Pompeian Red'.

To Mrs Patrick Campbell This poem is in a typescript dated 30 January

NOTES ON THE POEMS AND ESSAYS 133

1909. According to Suzanne Henig's essay 'Queen of Lud', HM studied at RADA under the actress Mrs Patrick Campbell in 1909. HM has made one handwritten correction in pencil by inserting 'vine' above the word 'crowned'.

To Jean, Who Loves Faerie-tales   Two slightly variant drafts of this poem are in manuscript. Jean may refer to Jessie Stewart's daughter, the literature scholar Jean Stewart Pace (1903–?), whom HM and Jessie often discussed in their correspondence.

The Moon-Flowers, Love, Carpe Diem, The Moon-Maid and *My Soul Was a Princess*   From an undated manuscript in Mirrlees's hand. Occasionally handwritten notes appear to have been made by an unidentified reader.

from *My Mother's Pedigree*   This poem is part of an unfinished draft about HM's mother Emily Lina Mirrlees, found in her notebooks. I have excerpted the first section of what appears to be draft in progress. HM also compiled a history of her maternal ancestors, the Moncrieff family, in the 1950s. A typescript of the Moncrieff family pedigree is among HM's papers. The poem links her mother's ancestry to famous figures from Scottish history. The caesura in line 21 was most likely unintentionally left by HM, who perhaps intended to return to complete the line at a later state.

The Faerie Changelings   Part of an incomplete typescript dated 1909.

'Some talk of Alexander and some sing Monty's praise...'   Part of an undated typescript. The poem refers to events and historical figures at the end of World War II. The first line is an echo of 'The British Grenadiers', the popular seventeenth-century marching song glorifying the grenadier units of the British army. 'Mappie' was the nickname given to HM's mother by her children.

A Friendship, The Shooting Stars, Ostia Antica and *The Toad*   Are all in typescript, in an envelope of HM's poems kept by Mary Lascelles. A note in HM's hand on the first page of this typescript: 'Some poems, written this summer and autumn – & not quite so gloom shadowed I think.' Ostia Antica is the harbour city of ancient Rome. HM was in Rome during late summer of 1959, so it is possible that these poems date from this period. In *Ostia Antica* 'smooths' has been corrected to 'smoothes'. *The Toad*: a 'knop' is a small knob.

The Invocation   This typescript is dated 8 March 1909. The original poem by the French writer and aristocrat Comtesse Anna de Noailles (1876–1933) appeared in the collection entitled *Les Éblouissements* (1907). With Karin Stephen, HM lunched with the Comtesse at her home in Paris in 1913, but would have been familiar with her poetry before their meeting. HM was fluent in French from an early age. For more information on Anna de Noailles, see Catherine Perry's *Persephone Unbound*. A discussion of 'Invocation' can be found on pp. 54, 141–2, 167–9, and 170. 'Salambô' refers to Gustave Flaubert's novel *Salammbô* (1862) and the allusion here is to the novel's enchanting eponymous heroine.

Dusk   Undated handwritten page, part of the same manuscript as 'The Moon-Flowers', 'Love', 'Carpe Diem', 'My Soul Was a Princess' and 'The Moon-Maid'. Samain (1858–1900) was a French Symbolist poet.

Essays

Some Aspects of the Art of Alexey Mikhailovich Remizov   The essay appeared in French translation as 'Quelques aspects de l'art d'Alexis Mikhailovich Rémizov', *Le Journal de Psychologie Normale et Pathelogique*, Jan–March 1926, 'Arts and Philosophy' issue, pp. 148–59. HM met the Russian writer Remizov (1877–1957) in Paris. He was a member of the Russian literary émigré community and helped JH and HM to translate *The Life of the Archpriest Avvakum by Himself* (1924). The two women also included some of Remizov's short stories in their collection of Russian folktales, *The Book of the Bear*, which was published in the same year as this article. HM and JH discuss Remizov's work in their introduction to *The Book of the Bear*. The English-language version of this article comes from two typescript drafts in HM's archive. The reproduced version is the draft labelled in HM's hand 'corrected version'. On p. 76 HM refers to the French writer and critic Charles Du Bos (1882–1939). She befriended him and his wife and attended the *décades* of Pontigny, which Du Bos hosted. He admired HM's second novel, *The Counterplot*, and facilitated the translation of a French edition. The quotations from Du Bos translate as 'the ether on which we are carried, it is not the message in itself but the wave that will transmit all possible messages, or, if you like, the envelope, the impalpable protective tunic that renders invulnerable and glorious any body of truth ready to rise up', and 'In it is found more light than real things, more of ideal forms than of matter.' I am grateful to Alfred Corn for these translations.

Listening in to the Past   From *The Nation & Athenaeum*, 11 September 1926, Vol. 39, pp. 670–71. '. . .the ship that was bringing the Queen from Norway': HM notes that 'It is a curious fact that the spells the witches confess to using, and the words with which their families greet them, are often Pater Nosters and Ave Marias. The Reformation came late to Scotland, and all these witches must have been baptised into the old faith; but, evidently, Papistry had already acquired the sinister terrifying atmosphere, the smell of incarnate evil, which can, I think, only be understood by such of us who have been brought up by a Scottish nurse.' HM has made three amendments to her personal copy of this article. 'Channing's voice booming out, "We must defend Portugal"', is replaced by 'Bossuet's voice, broken by sobs, as he intones "Madame meurt. Madam est morte."' *Paris* also makes mention of the historical figure Bossuet: 'Echoes of Bossuet chanting dead queens'; see Briggs's Commentary on *Paris*. HM corrects a description of a portrait 'casket' owned by Queen Elizabeth I: 'No – she kept a collection of miniatures in a cabinet. Cf. *Memoires* of Sir James Melville.' The only other alteration to the text is grammatical.

An Earthly Paradise   From *Time and Tide*, Miscellany, 25 February 1927, pp. 179–81. HM and her partner JH lived at the American Women's Club, 4 rue de Chevreuse, Paris from November 1922 to September 1925. The Club has since been renamed Reid Hall, after its benefactor, the American philanthropist and activist Elizabeth Mills Reid, and is still a centre for American university students. HM refers to 'a witty friend': this was Madame Duclaux, an English writer and scholar of French literature, better known as Mary Robinson (1857–1944). The Keller Institute, a Protestant school attended by André Gide in 1886, was originally housed on the premises of what is now Reid Hall. Gide discusses his experiences at 'Pension Keller' in his 1924 memoir *Si le grain ne meurt* (in English editions, *If It Die*), pp. 158–63. *Wide Wide World* (1850) by Susan Warner and Susan Coolidge's *What Katy Did* (1872) are both American novels that feature young female protagonists. Hope's use of the phrase 'Life with a capital L' (p. 93) may originate with JH. According to Hope, Jane was suspicious of certain nineteenth-century French poets who believed 'Life' was 'drinking vermouth in a Paris café'. Hope writes that Jane 'never would subscribe to the superstition that there was such a thing as life with a big L. "Life is life." she used to say.' For 'the principle of *suave mari*' (p. 93), see note to 'Bedside Books', below.

The Religion of Women   From *The Nation & Athenaeum*, 28 May 1927, Vol. 41, pp. 259–60. 'Time's wingèd chariot hurrying near' is a line from Andrew Marvell's poem 'To His Coy Mistress'.

Gothic Dreams   From *The Nation & Athenaeum*, 3 March 1928, Vol. 42, pp. 810–11. HM notes "The Haunted Castle': A Study of the Elements of English Romanticism by Eino Rialto.' She also notes at the end of the article: 'I am aware that "Christabel" and "Kubla Khan" were not actually published till 1816. But "Christabel", at any rate, was written very soon after "The Ancient Mariner."'

Bedside Books   From *Life & Letters*, June–December 1928, Vol. 1, pp. 562–74. 'Suave, mari magno turbantibus, aequora ventis, / E terra magnum alterius spectare laborem': 'It is sweet when on the great sea the winds trouble its waters, to behold from land another's deep distress'. The lines 'Apparet divum numen sedesque quieta...' translate as 'The divinity of the gods is revealed and their tranquil abodes, which neither winds do shake nor clouds drench with rains nor snow congealed by sharp frosts harms with hoary fall; an ever-cloudless ether o'ercanopies them, and they laugh with light shed largely round.' Both translations were included in footnotes to the original article, and are taken from Jane Harrison's *Art and Ritual* (1913). HM also footnotes 'we have heard it all hundreds of times before, and know the end as well as he' (p. 104): 'Cf., for instance, Bk. XII, IO *seq*.' On 'the other Democritus' (p. 106), HM notes: 'Democritus of Abdera, popularly known as the "Laughing

Philosopher", with whom, by writing under the pseudonym of "Democritus Junior", Burton associated himself, was the discoverer of the atomic theory, and hence, by way of Epicurus, the moulder of Lucretius's thought.'

Appendix

To Her. A twilight poem.

1
I have a little thing
Half-witting, huge of limb
And in the twilight dim
My song of her I sing.

2
She's common in her ways
By birth she's middle class
A Jew-Goy by descent
A sousy Scottish lass.

3
She has great bulging eyes
She has a красный нос
Which to my great surprise
Upon the sheet she blows.

4
Her speech too is obscene
And all the talk of her
It runs on Mrs Moon
And claustrophobia.

5
Her manners are so gross
That, not without just cause,
Against her I uplift
My soft slapping fur-paws.

6
Her body painful is

And hollow is her head
Like Dr Cranmer she
Doth scrabble in her bed.

7

Her name 'The Walrus' is
Twas given her no doubt
Because she neernoots in
And then she neernoots out.

8

And her small soft fur-paws
Are things to wonder at
They are like bits of stick
Stuck in a hump of fat.

9

A slow and heavy beast
She toiled thro' nights of pain
And days of haggard woe
At writing Madeleine.

10

Next at the Bear's soft speech
She toiled full many a day
The bright industrious frogs
They took it in their play
At last she worried thro'
And is a diplomée.

11

Her friend is Little-Sweet-Hole
Her lover is Huge Breast
With them she does indulge
In many a tedious jest.

12

And tedious is her speech
Thro all the livelong day
'Supposing' she will ask
'That some one were to stay'.

13

In all her bright young life
She has one only care
She never can bring forth
A small soft-yaller-Bear.

14

My husband chose her out
To be his concubine
His morganatic wife
And last – O joy divine
We dwell together free from strife
His younger and his elder wife.

15

Until at last we wend our ways
To far off peaceful Père-La-Chaise
In death an undivided Three
Together He and I and She
The Trinity in Unity.

by Jane Ellen Harrison
4 Sept 1921

'красный нос' translates from the Russian as 'red nose'. 'Neernoots' is the Russian phonetic spelling for 'deep sea diving', relating to 'The Walrus' in the same stanza. It might also more generally mean 'to immerse onself deeply', perhaps into some sort of intellectual pursuit.

Index of Titles and First Lines

Titles are in *italics*.

A Moon-Maid sat in her garden of dreams	62
A mother sometimes dreams of an old age	21
A well-found house, commodious, sweet, and clean	32
After the long summer, languid with sun	66
Amor Fati	45
At last the thing we feared has come on us	28
At times in the post-prandial solitude	36
Because the story of an Angel sent	43
Bertha frightens Miss Bates	33
Carpe Diem	61
The Copper-Beech in St. Giles' Churchyard	22
Crossed in Love	55
The Death of Cats and Roses	24
Delightedly, each, turning to the other	66
Did some old Chinese poet ever sing	24
A Doggerel Epitaph for My Little Dog, Sally	51
Dusk	70
Et in Arcadia Ego	26
The Faerie Changelings	64
Fresh, smiling, and domestic as a rose	33
A Friendship	66
From the vales of the moon, from the woods of the sea	64
The Glass Tánagra	30
God wrote His holy laws on stars and stones	45
Gulls	46
He said: 'I'd like to get into your dreams.'	55

Heart's city – listen while I sing to you – 'tis night	68
Heaven is Not Fairyland	45
Heaven is not Fairyland (alas!)	45
Here lies the dust of my small peke	51
I dreamt that I had wandered far away	30
I have no wish to eat forbidden fruit	26
I walked along St. Giles, passing the golden doors	22
I want a holophrase	3
I wish my library had got a skull!	25
I'd like to get into your dreams	55
If poets are to win to artistry	30
In a Pagan Wood	36
In that elusive hour that comes between	40
The Invocation	68
Is it presumptuous to suppose that love	55
Jesus Wept	52
The Land of Uz	28
The Legend of the Painted Room	30
Love	60
'Love lies bleeding' is the old song	56
Love Lies Dying	56
Maids dream of Love to be a mighty King	60
A Meditation on Donatello's Annunciation in the Church of Santa Croce, Florence	46
The Moon-Flowers	59
The Moon-Maid	62
Mothers	21
My mother had a maid called Barbara	52
from *My Mother's Pedigree*	63
My mother's pedigree	63
My Soul Was a Princess	61
My soul was a princess who dwelt in state	61
Now fountains play no more	67
Oh! May I make each moment of my life a gem	61
On the black ridge of the road	67
Ostia Antica	67

Paris: A Poem	3
A Portrait of the Second Eve, Painted in Pompeian Red	43
The Rendez-Vous	32
Sickness and Recovery at the Cape of Good Hope in Spring	37
The Shooting Stars	66
A Skull	25
'Some talk of Alexander and some sing Monty's praise'	65
Some talk of Alexander and some sing Monty's praise	65
The Angel of Dusk glides over the flowers	70
The gracious form of Greece died long ago	57
The moon-flowers white	59
The Protestants lie safe and snug in bed	46
The rosary's First Joyful Mystery	46
The sultry scene by Jacob's well when Christ	32
There's nothing lovelier than the Cape in spring	37
To Jean, Who Loves Faerie-tales	58
To Mrs Patrick Campbell	57
The Toad	67
'Une Maison Commode, Propre, et Belle...'	32
When people are small with curly hair	58
Winter Trees	40

FyfieldBooks

Two millennia of essential classics
The extensive FyfieldBooks list includes

Djuna Barnes *The Book of Repulsive Women and other poems*
edited by Rebecca Loncraine

Elizabeth Barrett Browning *Selected Poems* edited by Malcolm Hicks

Charles Baudelaire *Complete Poems in French and English*
translated by Walter Martin

Thomas Lovell Beddoes *Death's Jest-Book* edited by Michael Bradshaw

Aphra Behn *Selected Poems*
edited by Malcolm Hicks

Border Ballads: A Selection
edited by James Reed

The Brontë Sisters *Selected Poems*
edited by Stevie Davies

Sir Thomas Browne *Selected Writings*
edited by Claire Preston

Lewis Carroll *Selected Poems*
edited by Keith Silver

Paul Celan *Collected Prose*
translated by Rosmarie Waldrop

Thomas Chatterton *Selected Poems*
edited by Grevel Lindop

John Clare *By Himself*
edited by Eric Robinson and David Powell

Arthur Hugh Clough *Selected Poems*
edited by Shirley Chew

Samuel Taylor Coleridge *Selected Poetry* edited by William Empson and David Pirie

Tristan Corbière *The Centenary Corbière*
in French and English
translated by Val Warner

William Cowper *Selected Poems*
edited by Nick Rhodes

Gabriele d'Annunzio *Halcyon*
translated by J.G. Nichols

John Donne *Selected Letters*
edited by P.M. Oliver

William Dunbar *Selected Poems*
edited by Harriet Harvey Wood

Anne Finch, Countess of Winchilsea *Selected Poems*
edited by Denys Thompson

Ford Madox Ford *Selected Poems*
edited by Max Saunders

John Gay *Selected Poems*
edited by Marcus Walsh

Oliver Goldsmith *Selected Writings*
edited by John Lucas

Robert Herrick *Selected Poems*
edited by David Jesson-Dibley

Victor Hugo *Selected Poetry*
in French and English
translated by Steven Monte

T.E. Hulme *Selected Writings*
edited by Patrick McGuinness

Leigh Hunt *Selected Writings*
edited by David Jesson Dibley

Wyndham Lewis *Collected Poems and Plays* edited by Alan Munton

Charles Lamb *Selected Writings*
edited by J.E. Morpurgo

Lucretius *De Rerum Natura: The Poem on Nature*
translated by C.H. Sisson

John Lyly *Selected Prose and Dramatic Work*
edited by Leah Scragg

Ben Jonson *Epigrams and The Forest*
edited by Richard Dutton

Giacomo Leopardi *The Canti*
with a selection of his prose
translated by J.G. Nichols

Stéphane Mallarmé *For Anatole's Tomb*
in French and English
translated by Patrick McGuinness

Andrew Marvell *Selected Poems*
edited by Bill Hutchings

Charlotte Mew *Collected Poems and Selected Prose*
edited by Val Warner

Michelangelo *Sonnets*
translated by Elizabeth Jennings,
introduction by Michael Ayrton

William Morris *Selected Poems*
edited by Peter Faulkner

John Henry Newman *Selected Writings to 1845*
edited by Albert Radcliffe

Ovid *Amores*
translated by Tom Bishop

Fernando Pessoa *A Centenary Pessoa*
edited by Eugenio Lisboa and L.C. Taylor, introduction by Octavio Paz

Petrarch *Canzoniere*
translated by J.G. Nichols

Edgar Allan Poe *Poems and Essays on Poetry*
edited by C.H. Sisson

Restoration Bawdy
edited by John Adlard

Rainer Maria Rilke *Sonnets to Orpheus and Letters to a Young Poet*
translated by Stephen Cohn

Christina Rossetti *Selected Poems*
edited by C.H. Sisson

Dante Gabriel Rossetti *Selected Poems and Translations*
edited by Clive Wilmer

Sir Walter Scott *Selected Poems*
edited by James Reed

Sir Philip Sidney *Selected Writings*
edited by Richard Dutton

John Skelton *Selected Poems*
edited by Gerald Hammond

Charlotte Smith *Selected Poems*
edited by Judith Willson

Henry Howard, Earl of Surrey *Selected Poems*
edited by Dennis Keene

Algernon Charles Swinburne *Selected Poems*
edited by L.M. Findlay

Arthur Symons *Selected Writings*
edited by Roger Holdsworth

William Tyndale *Selected Writings*
edited by David Daniell

Oscar Wilde *Selected Poems*
edited by Malcolm Hicks

William Wordsworth *The Earliest Poems* edited by Duncan Wu

Sir Thomas Wyatt *Selected Poems*
edited by Hardiman Scott

For more information, including a full list of Fyfield*Books* and a contents list for each title, and details of how to order the books, visit the Carcanet website at www.carcanet.co.uk or email info@carcanet.co.uk